THIS PAGE:
Wolf Rock is made up of metamorphosed fluvial (river deposited) sediments of the Weverton Formation (Maryland Heights Member) in Catoctin Mountain Park NPS Photo by Gregory Gusse.

ON THE COVER:
Weathered rocks of the Weverton Formation (Maryland Heights Member) are also exposed at Chimney Rock within Catoctin Mountain Park. NPS Photo.

Catoctin Mountain Park

Geologic Resources Inventory Report

Natural Resource Report NPS/NRPC/GRD/NRR—2009/120

Geologic Resources Division
Natural Resource Program Center
P.O. Box 25287
Denver, Colorado 80225

August 2009

U.S. Department of the Interior
National Park Service
Natural Resource Program Center
Denver, Colorado

The Natural Resource Publication series addresses natural resource topics that are of interest and applicability to a broad readership in the National Park Service and to others in the management of natural resources, including the scientific community, the public, and the NPS conservation and environmental constituencies. Manuscripts are peer-reviewed to ensure that the information is scientifically credible, technically accurate, appropriately written for the intended audience, and is designed and published in a professional manner.

Natural Resource Reports are the designated medium for disseminating high priority, current natural resource management information with managerial application. The series targets a general, diverse audience, and may contain NPS policy considerations or address sensitive issues of management applicability. Examples of the diverse array of reports published in this series include vital signs monitoring plans; "how to" resource management papers; proceedings of resource management workshops or conferences; annual reports of resource programs or divisions of the Natural Resource Program Center; resource action plans; fact sheets; and regularly-published newsletters.

Views, statements, findings, conclusions, recommendations and data in this report are solely those of the author(s) and do not necessarily reflect views and policies of the U.S. Department of the Interior, National Park Service. Mention of trade names or commercial products does not constitute endorsement or recommendation for use by the National Park Service.

Printed copies of reports in these series may be produced in a limited quantity and they are only available as long as the supply lasts. This report is also available online from the Geologic Resources Inventory website (http://www.nature.nps.gov/geology/inventory/gre_publications) and the Natural Resource Publication Management website (http://www.nature.nps.gov/publications/NRPM/index.cfm) or by sending a request to the address on the back cover.

Please cite this publication as:

Thornberry-Ehrlich, T. 2009. Catoctin Mountain Park Geologic Resources Inventory Report. Natural Resource Report NPS/NRPC/GRD/NRR—2009/120. National Park Service, Denver, Colorado.

NPS 841/100133, August 2009

Contents

Figures

Executive Summary

This report accompanies the digital geologic map for Catoctin Mountain Park in Maryland, which the Geologic Resources Division produced in collaboration with its partners. It contains information relevant to resource management and scientific research. This document incorporates preexisting geologic information and does not include new data or additional fieldwork.

Catoctin Mountain Park is located in central Maryland, along the ridge that forms the boundary between the Blue Ridge and the Piedmont physiographic provinces. The rock in the park area reflects the tremendous tectonic forces that gave rise to the Appalachian Mountains. Precambrian gneisses, metamorphosed rocks, and younger (Paleozoic) quartzites and phyllites underlie the landscape. The entire region was compressed during three separate tectonic events: the Taconic, Acadian, and Alleghanian orogenies. The culmination of these events was the formation of the Blue Ridge-South Mountain anticlinorium. Catoctin Mountain is on the eastern limb of this large regional fold.

Originally established under the New Deal legislation of Franklin D. Roosevelt's presidential administration, the park was transferred to the National Park Service in 1936. Catoctin Mountain Park now covers 2,351 ha (5,810 acres) of hardwood forest, Blue Ridge Mountains, historic buildings and camps, and pristine waterways, and is part of a larger protected area that includes Cunningham Falls State Park, the Frederick and Thurmont watersheds, and Gambrill State Park. The park's landscape features are intimately connected with the long geologic history of the area. Thus, understanding the park's geologic history and resources is crucial to effective resource management, informing decisions related to geologic issues, future scientific research projects and interpretive needs.

Historically, the geology of the Catoctin Mountain Park area created a welcoming environment for human use. American Indians were attracted to the Catoctin area for tool making. Because of its fine-grained homogenous nature, metarhyolite rocks were ideal for making arrowheads, knifes, scrapers, and other implements. Springs served as important sources of water for both American Indians and settlers. Settlers made the area a focal point for hunting, mining, settlement, industry, and agriculture. To this day, the local geology inspires wonder in visitors and merits emphasis through interpretation.

Since the 1700s, humans have significantly modified the landscape and environment of Catoctin Mountain with dams, camps, buildings, roads, bridges, streamworks, and the impacts of air and water pollution. These actions have modified the dynamic geologic system that is capable of noticeable change within a human life span. Geological also processes continue to change the landscape. Balancing historical and natural preservation and restoration with recreation makes resource management a challenge. The following features, issues, and processes were identified as having geological importance and worthy of the highest level of management significance to the park:

- Geology and Biodiversity. The park is famous for its forest biodiversity, with successional hardwood forest now covering 95% of the park. This diversity is a direct result of the geology, topography, and climate of the area. Protecting these ecosystems—including streamside wetlands, hillslopes, and ridge tops—and understanding the relationships between geology and biology are key to effective resource management.
- Erosion and Slope Processes. The relatively wet climate of the eastern United States, combined with the severe storms, loose soils on steep slopes, and active streams at Catoctin Mountain Park, create slumping, slope creep, and streambank erosion issues. These problems are accelerated by a local lack of stabilizing plant growth in the thin, rocky, permeable, and easily disturbed soils. Runoff dramatically alters the landscape, creates new hazard areas in the process, and may clog streams with excess sediment that affects hydrologic systems and aquatic life.
- Water Issues. Big Hunting and Owens creeks drain the high annual precipitation at Catoctin Mountain Park. Water resources are under constant threat of contamination and overuse due to high visitation at the park and development in the surrounding areas. The most severe threats to park streams arise from human activities in the surrounding region, and include effects from road salts, septic systems, lagoon systems, fertilizers, farm animals, and acid rain. The combined result of these activities and natural lithologic controls can negatively alter groundwater chemistry.

Other issues, including recreational demands and general geological research, were also identified as critical management issues for Catoctin Mountain Park. These issues are listed in detail in the body of the report, along with recommendations for inventories, monitoring, and research. In addition, interpretative needs related to land use planning and visitor use in the park must be considered. A detailed geologic map, a road or trail log, and a guidebook that includes Catoctin Mountain Park and other parks in the Central Appalachian region will enhance visitor appreciation of the geologic history and dynamic processes that created the natural landscape showcased at the park. Strategically placed wayside interpretive exhibits will help interpret park geology for visitors.

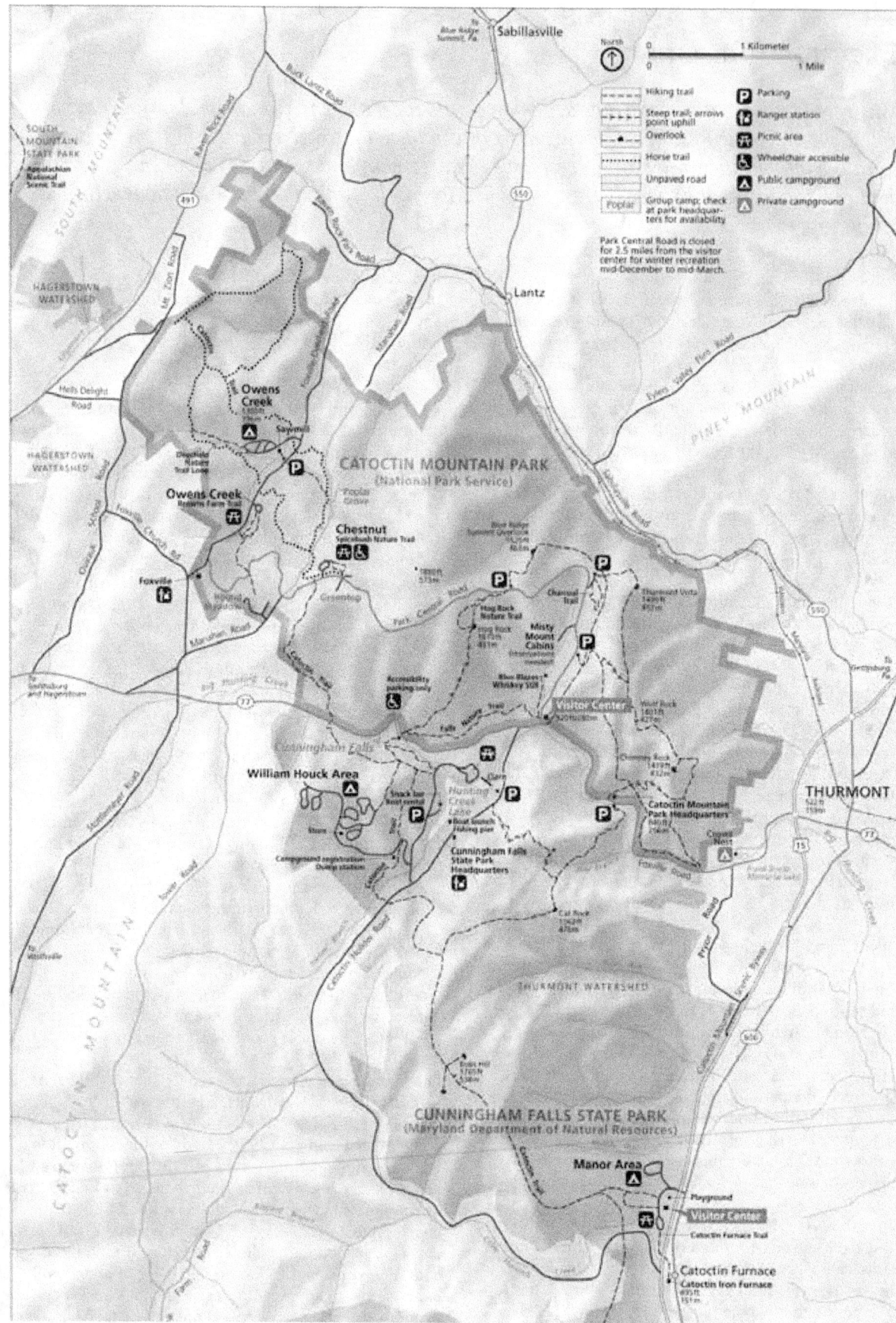

Figure 1. Map of features within Catoctin Mountain Park and surrounding areas. NPS map.

Introduction

The following section briefly describes the National Park Service Geologic Resources Inventory and the regional geologic setting of Catoctin Mountain Park.

Purpose of the Geologic Resources Inventory

The Geologic Resources Inventory (GRI) is one of 12 inventories funded under the National Park Service (NPS) Natural Resource Challenge designed to enhance baseline information available to park managers. The program carries out the geologic component of the inventory effort. The Geologic Resources Division of the Natural Resource Program Center administers this program. The GRI team relies heavily on partnerships with the U.S. Geological Survey, Colorado State University, state surveys, and others in developing GRI products.

The goal of the GRI is to increase understanding of the geologic processes at work in parks and provide sound geologic information for use in park decision making. Sound park stewardship relies on understanding natural resources and their role in the ecosystem. Geology is the foundation of park ecosystems. The compilation and use of natural resource information by park managers is called for in section 204 of the National Parks Omnibus Management Act of 1998 and in NPS-75, Natural Resources Inventory and Monitoring Guideline.

To realize this goal, the GRI team is systematically conducting a scoping meeting for each of the identified 270 natural area parks and providing a park-specific digital geologic map and geologic report. These products support the stewardship of park resources and are designed for nongeoscientists. Scoping meetings bring together park staff and geologic experts to review available geologic maps and discuss specific geologic issues, features, and processes.

The GRI mapping team converts the geologic maps identified for park use at the scoping meeting into digital geologic data in accordance with their innovative Geographic Information Systems (GIS) Data Model. These digital data sets bring an exciting interactive dimension to traditional paper maps by providing geologic data for use in park GIS and facilitating the incorporation of geologic considerations into a wide range of resource management applications. The newest maps come complete with interactive help files. This geologic report aids in the use of the map and provides park managers with an overview of park geology and geologic resource management issues.

For additional information regarding the content of this report and current GRI contact information please refer to the Geologic Resources Inventory Web site (http://www.nature.nps.gov/geology/inventory/).

History of Catoctin Mountain Park

Catoctin Mountain Park was originally established on January 7, 1935 as Catoctin Recreation Demonstration Area, as part of "The New Deal" legislation passed during Franklin D. Roosevelt's presidency. The park was transferred to the National Park Service on November 14, 1936 and renamed on July 12, 1954, and this redesignation accompanied a boundary change. Catoctin Mountain Park contains 2,351 hectares (5,810 acres) of hardwood forest, Blue Ridge Mountains, historic buildings and camps, and pristine waterways. The park is part of a larger protected area that includes Cunningham Falls State Park, the Frederick and Thurmont watersheds, and Gambrill State Park (fig. 1).

The area was set aside for restoration and preservation as a respite for the people living in the rapidly developing Washington, D.C. metro area just 97 km (60 mi) away. Camp David, the presidential retreat, is located within park boundaries. Catoctin Mountain was nearly devoid of trees after being subjected to years of agriculture and logging between 1776 and 1903. Much of this deforestation was conducted to provide timber and charcoal to fuel the iron industry at the Catoctin Furnace near Thurmont. Remains of the furnace are within Cunningham Falls State Park. Since then, many attempts have been made to restore the natural processes and features that were present at Catoctin Mountain prior to the environmental degradation of the 1800s and early 1900s, and to make the landscape accessible to the public. The Works Progress Administration (WPA), which was part of the New Deal, conducted the initial restoration efforts. The WPA was responsible for many of the historic structures within the park, including the central garage unit, the Blue Blazes Contact Station (now the park visitor center), the Project Headquarters (now the resource management center), and several camps.

Another New Deal program, the Civilian Conservation Corps (CCC), started work in the park on April 1, 1939. The CCC continued building camps and planting as many as 5,000 trees, including red maples, pitch pines, and other native species. CCC crews rehabilitated 320 ha (800 acres) of fields, improved Big Hunting Creek and Owens Creek, reclaimed old logging roads, dug the park's water system, and installed dry stone walls as part of the overall landscaping around the public facilities at the park.

Geologic Setting

Catoctin Mountain Park is located on the eastern slopes of Catoctin Mountain. The mountain is situated on the eastern limb of the Blue Ridge-South Mountain anticlinorium as part of the northern end of the Blue Ridge, a physiographic province of the Appalachian

Mountains (fig. 2). The mountain forms the easternmost portion of the Blue Ridge province of Maryland and northern Virginia as a belt of Lower Cambrian sediments and older metamorphosed volcanic rocks. Immediately east of Catoctin Mountain Park is the normal fault boundary between the Blue Ridge and Piedmont provinces (described below). The mountain ridge extends some 80 km (50 mi) along a discontinuous, linear, northeast-southwest trend from Emmitsburg, Maryland to Leesburg, Virginia. The width of the mountain ranges from 3 to 6 km (2 to 4 mi) in Maryland to less than 1.6 km (1 mi) in Virginia.

Frederick Valley, underlain by Triassic sediments (of the Mesozoic Gettysburg basin), sits east of the park. Middleton Valley, underlain by metamorphosed volcanic rocks (Whitaker 1955), lies west of the park. Hunting Creek separates the park from the main ridge in the south, while Owens Creek provides separation to the west, north, and east.

The topography within the park consists of rolling hills and narrow ridgetops separated by steep-sloped valleys and ravines. The landscape at Catoctin Mountain Park is largely a function of the different types of underlying bedrock. The ridgetops are composed of resistant late Precambrian (Neoproterozoic) to early Paleozoic metamorphic rocks of the Catoctin Formation and Chilhowee Group (Loudoun, Weverton, Harpers, and Antietam formations). The Catoctin Formation contains metamorphosed volcanic rocks associated with ancient continental rifting. The quartz-rich rocks of the Chilhowee Group began as fluvial sediments deposited atop the volcanic rocks. Valleys separate the ridgetops now that less resistant units have eroded. Relief varies from lower elevations of approximately 244 m (800 ft) above sea level near Camp Peniel to nearly 488 m (1,600 ft) at Hog Rock and 573 m (1,880 feet) at Camp 3 (Trombley and Zynjuk 1985). Catoctin Mountain rises to 579 m (1,900 ft) outside the park.

Several of the physiographic provinces relevant to the geologic history of Catoctin Mountain Park are described below from east to west (fig 2.).

Piedmont Province

The rocks of the eastward-sloping Piedmont Plateau formed through a combination of folding, faulting, uplifting, and metamorphism. The Piedmont is composed of hard, crystalline, igneous, and metamorphic rocks such as schists, phyllites, slates, gneisses, and gabbros. Valley incision by streams, rock weathering to depths of more than 15 km (9 mi) beneath hilltops, and slope erosion have resulted in an eastern landscape of gently rolling hills that start at an elevation of 60 m (200 ft) above sea level and become gradually steeper toward the western edge of the province at 300 m (1,000 ft).

Within the Piedmont are a series of Mesozoic-age extensional basins. A depositional contact, best indicated by a topographic change from the rolling hills of the Piedmont to relatively flat ground within the basin defines the boundary of the basins with the Piedmont Plateau. Each basin, formed by normal faults during crustal extension (the Earth's crust pulling apart), is superposed on the rocks and structure of the Piedmont. The faults opened basins (grabens), and the basins rapidly filled with roughly horizontal layers of sediment.

Blue Ridge Province

The Blue Ridge province extends from Georgia to Pennsylvania along the eastern edge of the Appalachian Mountains. Rocks of the Blue Ridge province in North Carolina feature the highest elevations in the Appalachian Mountain system. Precambrian and Paleozoic igneous and metamorphic rocks were uplifted during several orogenic events, and then deeply eroded to form the steep rugged terrain. The dominant structure of the Blue Ridge province in central Maryland is the Blue Ridge-South Mountain anticlinorium (fig. 3). Quartz-rich and erosion-resistant metamorphic rocks form the heights of Blue Ridge, Bull Run Mountain, South Mountain, and Hogback Ridge, whereas less resistant metamorphic rocks underlie the valleys. South Mountain and Catoctin Mountain, both anticlines, are two examples of the pervasive folding in the Blue Ridge province. Eroding streams have caused the narrowing of the northern section of the Blue Ridge Mountains into a thin band of steep ridges, climbing to heights of more than 1,200 m (3,900 ft).

Valley and Ridge Province

Long parallel ridges separated by valleys (100 to 200 m [330 to 660 ft] deep) characterize the landscape of the Valley and Ridge physiographic province (fig. 3). The landforms are strongly representative of the lithology and structure of the deformed bedrock; valleys formed in easily eroded shale and carbonate formations among more erosion-resistant sandstone ridges. The province contains strongly folded and faulted sedimentary rocks in western Maryland. The eastern portion is part of the Great Valley (locally referred to as Hagerstown Valley); this section is composed of rolling lowland formed on folded carbonate rocks and shale. The folded rocks are part of the west limb of the Blue Ridge-South Mountain anticlinorium.

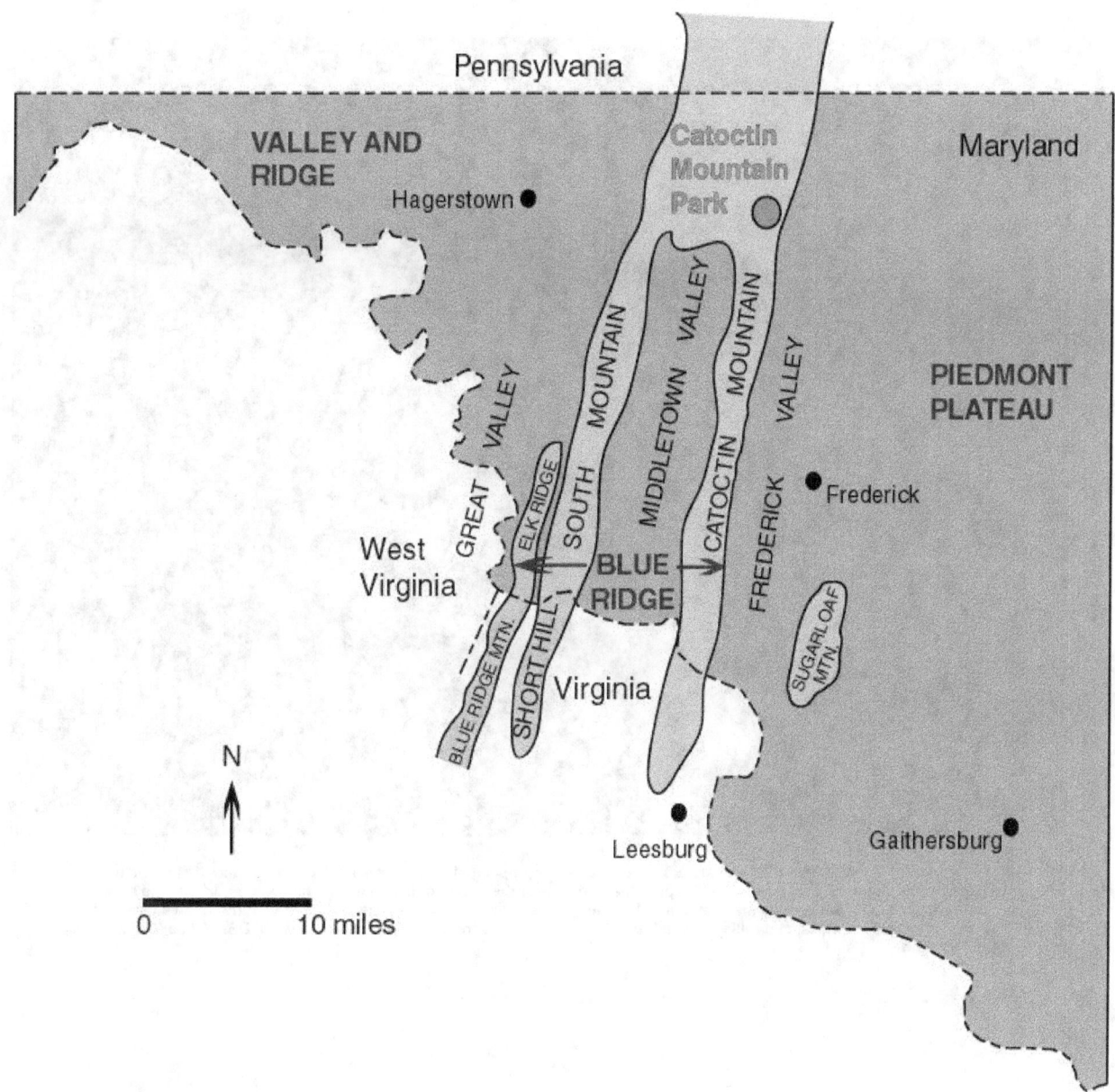

Figure 2. Location of Catoctin Mountain Park relative to geologic features of the Blue Ridge province in Maryland. Note also the locations of the Piedmont and Valley and Ridge provinces. Graphic adapted from a figure in Whitaker (1955).

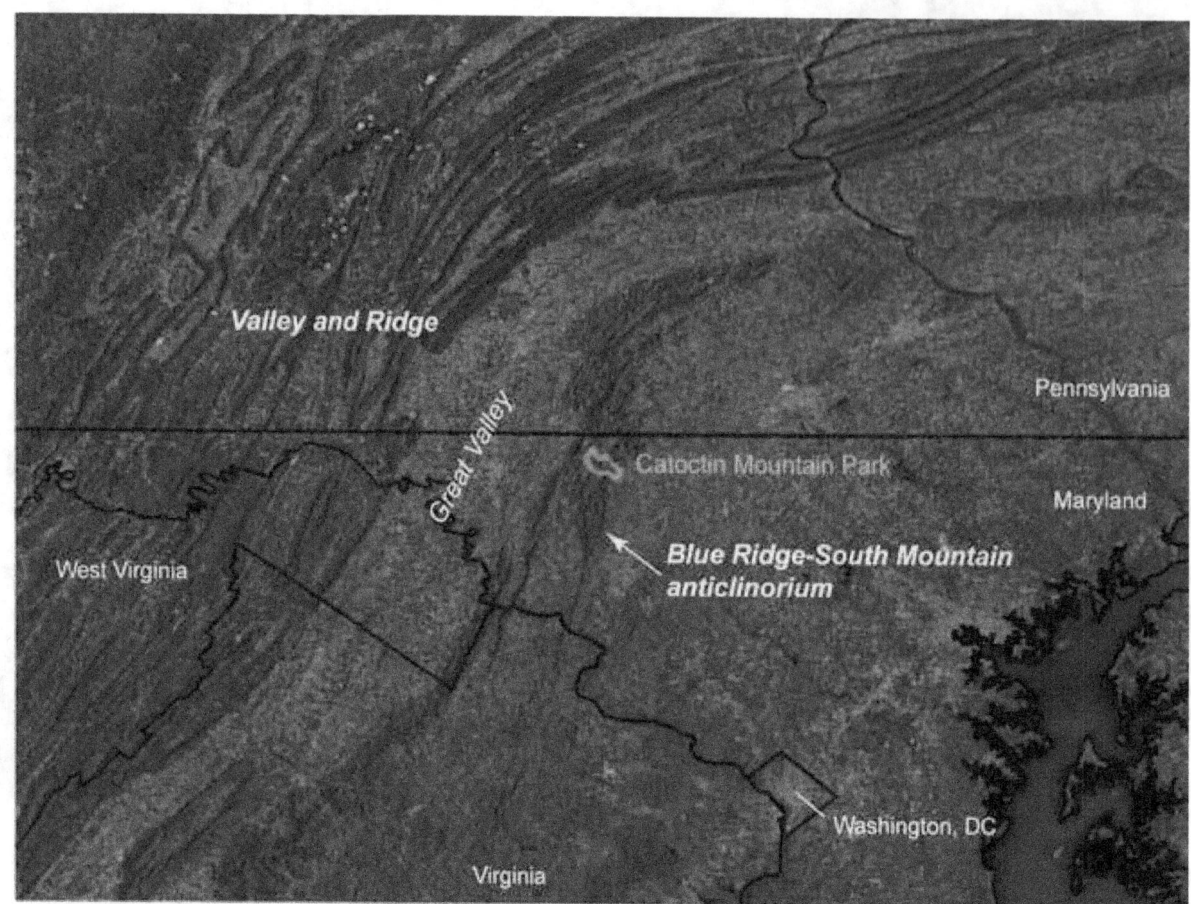

Figure 3. Aerial imagery illustrating folded and faulted landforms of the Appalachian Mountains surrounding Catoctin Mountain Park. The Blue Ridge-South Mountain anticlinorium is the prominent feature in the center of the image, its limbs extending to the southwest. The anticlinorium represents the northernmost extent of the Blue Ridge province. West of the park are the numerous valleys and ridges that characterize the aptly named Valley and Ridge province. Compiled from ESRI Arc Image Service, USA Prime Imagery. Image courtesy Thom Curdts (NPS).

Geologic Issues

The Geologic Resources Division held a Geologic Resources Inventory scoping session for Catoctin Mountain Park on April 30 – May 2, 2001, to discuss geologic resources, address the status of geologic mapping, and assess resource management issues and needs. This section synthesizes the scoping results, in particular those issues that may require attention from resource managers.

Geology and Biodiversity

Natural areas provide refuge for many species, and serve as rest stops for wildlife during movement or migration. Natural areas also serve as "living classrooms" for the public. Small national parks such as Catoctin Mountain Park add to the biological diversity of a region, and assume special importance in regions of heavy development like the Washington, D.C. metro area.

These small parks are often critical natural areas within dissected landscapes. Knowing the features responsible for the biodiversity at the parks—including geology, climate, topography, and hydrogeologic systems—is critical in understanding the parks' unique habitats and ecosystems. This knowledge allows for effective resource management.

Catoctin Mountain was not always the natural haven it is today. In the 1700s and 1800s, logging removed the thick hardwood forests from the slopes of Catoctin Mountain to produce charcoal for the iron works furnaces nearby. In addition, local agricultural practitioners cleared fields and slopes. According to the Frederick County Soil Survey, the soils of Catoctin Mountain are thin and rocky (Matthews 1960). The poorly developed, well-drained soils contain abundant stones and boulders throughout their profile. The stony soils were typically not conducive to repeat farming, and new fields were cleared of forest every year. No tree larger than a fence post existed when the National Park Service acquired the land in 1935 (Means 1995).

Soils on the eastern slope of Catoctin Mountain within and surrounding the park were derived from erosion of the Weverton Formation (quartzite). They are acidic, thin, sandy loams with high permeability, and support chestnut oak and pitch pine. In contrast, soils derived from the Catoctin Formation (greenstone), typical on the western side of the park, are deeper and more moist, orange, clayey, and rich in calcium and magnesium (Southworth and Denenny 2006). They can support a wider variety of tree species, including sugar maple, basswood, hickories, white ash, beech, and tulip poplar (Means 1995). These dissimilarities in soils, controlled by the parent rock type, cause differences in the distribution of vegetation.

Many forest ecosystems are present in the upland areas of the park. These ecosystems are controlled by the underlying geology. The park is 95% covered by hardwood forest, most of which is a secondary succession forest (Mid-latitude Deciduous Forest) containing a mix of oaks, hickories, tulip poplars, and maples. Tree species found locally include cherry, sassafras, elm, butternut, locust, walnut, hemlock, white pine, ash, and table mountain pine (NPS Web page http://www.nps.gov/cato). A unique opportunity exists to track the distribution of these forest species based on the geologic substrate (soil and rocks) because relatively few geologic units underlie Catoctin Mountain Park.

The substrate type and the geological features of the Blue Ridge (Catoctin Mountain)—including the ridges, ravines, steep slopes, and narrow stream valleys—are major determining factors for the flora and fauna protected within the park. The ecosystems can change dramatically depending on the facing direction of a particular ridge, elevation, soil type and permeability, degree of slope fluctuations, and exposure to climate and wind.

Wetlands are interspersed with the forest environments at Catoctin Mountain Park. Wetlands sustain significant biodiversity and are vital components of healthy ecosystems. They provide unique habitat, help control erosion and regulate flooding, and recharge groundwater and streamflow in drought years. Wetlands also act as natural filters for impurities and pollution in the water. To be classified as a wetland, an area must meet three criteria: (1) include hydric soils (be waterlogged for at least 1 to 2 weeks per year); (2) contain more than 50% of its total vegetation as designated wetland plants; and (3) possess signs of hydrology, including, but not limited to, drift lines, flow patterns, flood-related tree debris, and muddy substrate. There are 18 wetland areas at Catoctin Mountain Park, covering nearly 58 ha (143 acres) adjacent to streams. Matching the distribution of wetlands with landform and geologic substrate will increase awareness for subsequent restoration projects in the park.

Because geology forms the basis of the entire ecosystem, correlation of geological features with resources should be part of any biological inventory and monitoring effort to better predict occurrences and manage existing biological resources.

Inventory, Monitoring, and Research Recommendations for Geology and Biodiversity

- Measure and document changes in the hydrologic regime in impacted areas of the park, including roadways, trails, and visitor and administrative facilities.

- Identify and utilize reference sites for rare and significant habitats in an attempt to accurately restore the environment at Catoctin Mountain Park.
- Perform studies on forest regeneration rates and determine if geologic factors play a controlling role. Detailed geologic maps correlated with vegetation distribution are crucial to this task.
- Compile data for vascular plants and vertebrates with attention to geographic distribution. Sources include museum records of voucher specimens, previous studies, park databases, and other records.
- Study any geological influences on native and secondary habitat and species distribution, especially concerning soil/map unit (substrate) type. One application could be the relationship of the threatened purple fringed orchid's habitat to the underlying geology, and incorporate the orchid habitat locations into a GIS.
- Monitor changes to geologic factors controlling species distribution, including hydrologic systems, slopes, recent deposition, and sedimentation.
- Determine the extent to which park vegetation affects water quality leaving the park. Forests help filter nutrients and sediment, stabilize soils, and moderate flooding. Use this information to promote increased standards for water quality and responsible use of water resources.

Erosion and Slope Processes

The topographic differences within and surrounding the park can be high due to the rugged terrain. This is especially true along the banks of Big Hunting and Owens creeks and their tributaries. Most slopes in the park area are between 10% and 20%, and may be as high as 60% in some deeper ravines (Trombley and Zynjuk 1985). The likelihood of landslides increases with precipitation and undercutting of slopes by streams, roads, trails, and other development in addition to natural erosion. The relative potential (risk) for landslide occurrence could be assessed by using the following information sources: a topographic map to determine the steepness of a slope; a geologic map to determine the rock type; and recent rainfall data.

Severe weather, such as the microburst that struck in 1998 and destroyed nearly 1.5 ha (4 acres) of forest, is difficult to predict. This area of Maryland can receive large snowfalls such as the 208 cm (82 in) that fell in 1996, and it is located within a hurricane-affected zone. The extreme weather that occurs in this area—combined with the steep slopes, loose and unconsolidated soils, and substrate—can lead to sudden catastrophic slope failures. Rocks and soil can mobilize and slide downhill to cause a massive slump or debris flow, which can lead to shoreline erosion near streams and rivers, increased sediment load, gullying, and threat of destruction for trails, bridges, and other features of interest.

The average discharge of Big Hunting Creek is 0.08 to 0.14 m^3/sec (3 to 5 ft^3/sec) per second, or 83 to 144 liters (22 to 38 gallons) per second (Means 1995). Stream velocity varies according to the streambed width, surface, and gradient, but it is fastest near the middle of the stream. This differential in velocity creates erosive eddies that suspend material to be deposited in calmer water. Sediment load is a direct measure of the local amount of erosion on any given stream.

Increased erosion leads to increased sediment load within the park's rivers. Sediment loads and distribution affect aquatic and riparian ecosystems, and sediment loading can result in changes to channel morphology and increased overbank-flooding frequency. Increased erosion along the outer portions of bends in streambeds (where stream velocity is higher) can cause the banks to retreat, and undercutting of the banks can lead to washout, undermining the trees, trails, and other features along these banks. Trees can fall across the stream, and the trails can wash away. Measures are being taken to control such erosion at Catoctin Mountain Park. Cribbing, log frame deflectors, jack dams, stone riprap, and/or log dams are used to shore up the bank, deflect the flow, and slow erosion (Means 1995).

Inventory, Monitoring, and Research Recommendations for Erosion and Slope Processes

- Use shallow (~25 cm, 10 in) and deeper core data to monitor rates of sediment accumulation and erosion in the river, local streams, and springs. Analyze changes in chemical constituents of sediments as well as maximum flow.
- Monitor hazards from unstable slopes and streambanks.
- Monitor erosion rates by establishing key sites for repeated profile measurements to document rates of erosion or deposition and, if possible, measure shortly after major storms have occurred. Repeat photography may be useful.
- Comprehensively study the erosion/weathering processes active at the park, taking into account the different compositions of sediment deposits versus slope aspects, location, and likelihood of instability.
- Inventory areas susceptible to runoff flooding (paleoflood hydrology), and relate to climate and confluence areas.
- Perform trail stability studies and determine which trails are most at risk and in need of further stabilization.
- Perform channel morphology studies in relation to intense seasonal runoff. Consult professional geomorphologists concerning erosional processes.
- Inventory current channel morphological characteristics and monitor changes in channel morphology.
- Conduct a hydrologic-conditions assessment to identify actual and potential "problem reaches" for prioritized monitoring. Monitor with repeat aerial photographs once the problem reaches are identified.

Water Issues

The moist eastern climate of Maryland provides water for streams, rivers, runoff, springs, and groundwater wells. Annual precipitation at Catoctin Mountain Park averages 112 cm (44 in), with most of the rain coming in brief storms during the summer months. Water resources are under constant threat of contamination and overuse from existing and future development in the surrounding areas. The most severe threats to park streams are due to the impacts of this rapid growth in the region. Anthropogenic effects from road salts, septic systems, lagoon systems, fertilizers, farm animal waste, and acid rain can negatively alter groundwater chemistry (Trombley and Zynjuk 1985; Dyer and Logan 1995).

Preserving the integrity of the watershed is a major management objective at Catoctin Mountain Park. Differences in water quality stem from a variety of natural and non-natural sources. For instance, major geochemical differences exist between water sampled from areas underlain by different lithologic units as controlled by hydrolysis, the process that controls the chemical composition of most natural waters (Bowser and Jones 2002). Quartzite and phyllite near the crest of the mountain react differently with water than do the metabasalts along the slopes of the mountain. Water sampled from higher in the flow system showed higher sodium:calcium and sodium:magnesium ratios and lower pH, which reflects the more felsic (containing a higher percentage of lighter colored minerals) composition of the underlying geology there. Thinner soils and higher saprolite (clay-rich "decomposed" rock resulting from chemical weathering) content in some areas also affect water chemistry (Dyer and Logan 1995).

The two primary high-gradient streams in the park are Big Hunting Creek and Owens Creek. Studies of nearby streams have provided information on the interplay between geology and water chemistry in the area. Based on studies of Hauver Branch and Hunting Creek, surface water composition appears to vary seasonally. When the water level drops below the groundwater-bedrock surface in greenstone-dominated lithologies (abundant chlorite, epidote, albite, actinolite with scant calcite, quartz, potassium feldspar, and biotite minerals), the concentrations of calcium, magnesium, sodium, alkalinity, and silica increase, whereas the concentration of sulfite decreases (Bowser and Jones 2002).

Studies stress the importance of well-characterized mineral compositions for both the aqueous phase and the host rock. Groundwater chemistry in silicate-dominated lithologies seems particularly sensitive to compositions of plagioclase (albite), smectite (clay), and mafic minerals (mica, amphibole, and pyroxene), whereas the presence of quartz and/or potassium feldspar has very little effect (Logan and Kivimaki 1998; Bowser and Jones 2002). Similarly, it was determined that vein calcite and dolomite contribute calcium to the system and that chlorite contributes magnesium (Logan and Dyer 1996). Many of these minerals contributing to groundwater chemical variations would be present in the map units at Catoctin Mountain Park.

The park does not contain within its boundaries any watersheds in their entirety; however, Owens Creek's headwaters are located in the park and are relatively safe from contamination by outside sources. The sewage treatment plant near these headwaters must be carefully monitored to prevent contamination. Several streams along Catoctin Mountain, including Hauver Branch and Big Hunting Creek, are referred to as part of a "calibrated watershed" by various federal, state, and local entities. This reference resulted from a study that focused on understanding the acid-rain effect on weathering in the United States (Katz et al. 1985). Results from that study indicate that the watersheds at Catoctin Mountain are relatively clean, and they are cited as examples of pristine, unspoiled watersheds. However, issues still exist with regard to the health of the streams and lakes in the park. Suburban development surrounding Catoctin Mountain, emanating from the Washington, D.C. metro area, negatively affects the watersheds.

Where agricultural remnants, construction materials, and other human waste are present, nitrogen (and other contaminant) levels in the water may reach dangerous levels. Runoff from roadways often contains high levels of oil and other car emissions that flow to park waterways and seep into the soil. Salt used to keep roads clear of snow and ice in winter contaminates soils along ditches. To effectively protect the park's watershed ecosystem requires an awareness of the chemicals used in regional agriculture and development and an understanding of the hydrogeologic system (including groundwater flow patterns).

The framework for the groundwater flow system in the park is composed of weathered and fractured bedrock overlain by highly permeable, rocky soils and regolith. The thickness of the regolith (the primary groundwater reservoir) depends on the local topography. The reservoir is thickest in draws and valleys and thinnest along ridges and hilltops. The groundwater in the regolith, in contrast to that found in the fractures in the bedrock, is considered unconfined. However, the hydraulic connectivity between the bedrock and the regolith is high, which allows the entire system to be considered a complex unconfined aquifer (Trombley and Zynjuk 1985).

The movement of nutrients and contaminants through the ecosystem can be modeled by monitoring the composition of system inputs such as rainfall and outputs such as streamflow. Other input sources include wind, surface runoff, groundwater transport, sewage outfall, landfills, and fill dirt. Streams integrate the surface runoff and groundwater flow of their watersheds, thus providing a cumulative measure of the status of a watershed's hydrologic system. Consistent measurement of nutrients and contaminants is crucial to establishing baselines for comparison.

The hydrogeologic system changes in response to increased surface runoff. This increase is a result of the further development of impervious surfaces such as parking lots, roads, and buildings. Sedimentation also increases due to land clearing for development. Water temperature increases because of the insulating nature of impervious surfaces. Runoff from a parking lot on a hot July day is at a much higher temperature than runoff from a grassy slope.

Inventory, Monitoring, and Research Recommendations for Water Issues

- Establish working relationships with the U.S. Geological Survey and the Maryland Geological Survey, as well as local and national conservation groups, to study and monitor the park's watershed and the hydrology of the area for applications in hydrogeology, slope creep, streambank erosion, and other geologic hazards.
- Apply a mass transfer and/or balance model with a forward-modeling approach to the ground and surface water at the park to quantify lithologic controls on water chemistry (Bowser and Jones 2002).
- Map and quantify water subterranean recharge zones.
- To further characterize the health of the watersheds, continue studies of metals analysis; nitrite/nitrate, phosphate, and sulfate measurements; temporal analysis of dissolved oxygen; conductivity; pH; water temperature; bacterial concentrations; pesticide contamination; turbidity; and sediment load.
- Determine sources of runoff pollutants and sediments.
- Install monitoring stations around the park boundaries to measure atmospheric inputs of important chemical components (such as nitrogen, mercury, and pH) and outputs to streams and groundwater.
- Expand the scope of the water quality monitoring program (which started in 1978) to include additional sites within the park and to consider the geologic substrate and vegetation distribution (macro-invertebrate communities).

Recreational Demands

The two primary goals of the National Park Service are to: (1) protect park resources; and (2) provide opportunities for visitors to enjoy those resources. Catoctin Mountain Park provides numerous recreational opportunities, including hiking, fishing, climbing, cross country skiing, sledding, cabin and tent camping, bicycling, picnicking, and photography. The park promotes activities that do not damage the park's resources or endanger other visitors.

The park experiences high visitation, especially during the summer months. At least 466,926 people entered the park in FY2008. Visitors place increasing demands on the resources of the park, and management concerns range from trail erosion to climbing accidents.

Many trails wind through preserved biological, historical, and geological environments at the park. Several of the trails are especially fragile, and off-trail hiking promotes their degradation. According to the Soil Survey of Frederick County, the soils in the park are thin, well-drained, and rocky, and they lack significant vegetation for stability (Matthews 1960). Exposure of these soils on a slope renders them highly susceptible to erosion and degradation. The park attempts to concentrate the impacts of recreation by designating trails, camps, and picnic areas. Prohibited use in non-designated areas increases the area of impact and places delicate ecosystems at risk for contamination from waste.

Several streams, including Big Hunting Creek and Owens Creek, enhance the natural beauty of the park. As with hiking, overuse of certain areas can lead to contamination from waste and degradation of the ecosystem, and to increased stream edge erosion. The park has built buttresses on reaches of the creek where it approaches a visitor trail. These supports reduce streambank erosion, but such measures are temporary.

The rock outcrops of both the Weverton Formation and Catoctin Formation attract recreational climbers to the park. Features such as Chimney Rock and Wolf Rock (figs. 4 and 5) are ideal sites for climbing routes. However, Wolf Rock is currently the only location in the park where climbing is allowed (permit required). These recreational opportunities cause resource management concerns at Catoctin Mountain Park. The jointed and fractured rocks may fail, causing climbers to fall or to precipitate rockfall down the underlying slopes, which could injure other climbers. Slope erosion increases in areas of heavy climbing.

Inventory, Monitoring, and Research Recommendations for Recreational Demands

- Develop resource management plans, including inventory and monitoring, to further identify human impacts on any springs, wetlands, and marsh flora within the park.
- Design wayside exhibits to encourage responsible use of park resources.
- Determine a safe balance between rock climbing in the park, visitor safety and resource integrity.
- Promote stabilizing vegetation along slopes at risk for slumping and erosion.
- Determine the nature of potential geologic hazards that may exist along Route 77 near Big Hunting Creek.
- Promote topographic/geologic mapping in the park linked to recreational use patterns to determine areas at high risk for resource degradation.

General Geology and Miscellaneous Action Items

Inventory, Monitoring, and Research Recommendations for General Geology

- Monitor air quality, noise pollution levels, visibility, water quality, and viewshed quality, with attention to nearby industrial pollution, smog, and acid rain. Cooperate with local business and conservation groups to reduce pollution and promote appropriate development. The NPS Air Resources Division can provide assistance with this type of monitoring.
- Research fire history, behavior, and effects to build a knowledge base and implement a fire management plan that allows natural processes to keep the forest ecosystem healthy. Determine what, if any, effects fires will have on slope stability, and target potentially problematic areas for further protection and reinforcement.
- Cooperate in mapping wetlands with the NPS Water Resources Division.
- Relate topographic aspect and digital elevation models to the geology.

- Research the surficial geologic story at Catoctin Mountain and develop an interpretive program to relate the current landscape, ecosystem, and biology to the geology.
- Collaborate with other agencies, including the U.S. Geological Survey and the Maryland Geological Survey, to complete digital topographic and detailed geologic mapping in the area.
- Perform detailed geologic mapping within the park to determine the exact nature of the boundary between the Catoctin Formation and the Loudoun and Weverton formations.
- Promote interpretive exhibits to educate the public about the tectonic history of the eastern United States.
- Develop an interpretive exhibit discussing the geologic features (sedimentary deposits, igneous rocks, deformational structures, metamorphism) underlying the park, their origins, and their significance to the history of the area, especially concerning the regional historic iron extraction.

Figure 4. View from Chimney Rock, an outcrop of the Weverton Formation, within Catoctin Mountain Park. NPS Photo.

Figure 5. Wolf Rock, within Catoctin Mountain Park, is being wedged apart by plant roots and frost wedging. NPS Photo.

Geologic Features and Processes

This section describes the most prominent and distinctive geologic features and processes in Catoctin Mountain Park.

Blue Ridge-South Mountain Anticlinorium

The Blue Ridge province, composed primarily of allochthonous rock, reaches its northern terminus north of Catoctin Mountain in southern Pennsylvania. The Blue Ridge-South Mountain anticlinorium marks the easternmost extent of the Blue Ridge province in Maryland. It extends southwestward nearly 400 km (250 mi) to the Roanoke, Virginia area (Mitra 1989). The anticlinorium has three limbs from east to west: Catoctin Mountain; Black Oak Ridge-Short Hill-South Mountain; and Blue Ridge-Elk Ridge (Southworth et al. 2007). Catoctin Mountain Park is located on the eastern upright limb of the anticlinorium (figs. 2 and 3). The eastern limb of the anticlinorium at Catoctin Mountain exhibits open folds with uniform strains (Mitra 1976). The axial surface of the anticlinorium is inclined moderately to the southeast and plunges at a low angle to the northeast (Southworth and Denenny 2006).

The entire structure is locally overturned to the northwest (imagine the shape of an "A" leaning over and deformed to the left—west—as in fig. 11). The west limb dips steeply southeastward; the crest is broad and flat; and the east limb, where Catoctin Mountain Park is located, dips approximately 50° southeast. The rocks of Catoctin Mountain Park are within second-order folds that are inclined northwest up the east limb (Southworth and Denenny 2006). In the core of the anticlinorium, west of the park, some of the oldest rocks (more than 1,000 million [one billion] years old) in the Appalachians are exposed. These granodiorites and granitic gneisses (igneous and metamorphic rocks) are associated with the Grenville Orogeny described in the "Geologic History" section. Rocks of the core are flanked on each side by Precambrian and Lower Paleozoic metamorphosed sedimentary and metamorphosed volcanic rocks (Mitra 1989). The Swift Run (phyllites and quartzites) and Catoctin (greenstone, metamorphosed rhyolite, and metamorphosed sediments) formations unconformably overlie the Precambrian gneissic rocks in central Maryland (Onasch 1986). The anticlinorium is associated with thrust faulting during the Alleghanian Orogeny along a fault plane that extends eastward beneath the Piedmont Plateau province (fig. 11; Onasch 1986).

Structures along the limbs of the anticlinorium suggest multiple phases of deformation and metamorphism. The anticlinorium formed during the Alleghanian Orogeny in the Paleozoic. However, several phases of folding predate the greenschist (low-grade) metamorphism associated with the Alleghanian Orogeny, and therefore may represent deformation during the Taconic or Acadian orogenies described in the "Geologic History" section (Onasch 1986). Mineral assemblages present in the Catoctin Formation phyllites—namely muscovite, chlorite, and chloritoid—suggest temperatures of metamorphism between 350° and 420° C (660° and 790° F) and pressures of metamorphism at approximately 3.5 kilobars (more than 3,500 times atmospheric pressure at the Earth's surface). The folding and thrusting of the Blue Ridge rocks were accompanied by a strong cleavage (parting) in the rocks. This cleavage and associated fractures strike northeast and dip approximately 45° to the southeast, indicating different orientations of movement and deformation within the structure (Trombley and Zynjuk 1985).

The structure at Catoctin Mountain is truncated on the east by a Triassic-age border fault. The fault separates the early Paleozoic rocks to the west from the relatively undeformed sedimentary Triassic rocks filling the Frederick Valley. The fault is mostly covered by debris and sediments eroded from Catoctin Mountain (Whitaker 1955). The fault was active during the Triassic extension that was responsible for many large narrow northeast oriented, down-faulted basins along the foothills of the Appalachians following the Alleghanian Orogeny. The Culpeper Basin, south of Catoctin Mountain in Virginia, is another example of a Triassic extensional basin.

Catoctin Greenstone

Catoctin greenstone is the informal name for the metamorphosed basalt/volcanic breccia part of the widespread Catoctin Formation that also includes phyllites, metamorphosed rhyolite, and associated metamorphosed sedimentary rocks. A greenstone is defined as any compact, dark-green, altered or metamorphosed basic igneous rock with a typical mineral assemblage of chlorite, actinolite, and/or epidote. In outcrop, these rocks appear dark green.

The Catoctin greenstones are composed of metamorphosed basalt lava flows containing vesicles and irregular pods of light green epidosite (a metamorphic rock with quartz and epidote minerals), a result of hydrothermal alteration (Southworth and Denenny 2006). The metamorphosed basalt flows crop out along Park Central Road and at Cunningham Falls (Southworth and Denenny 2006). These massive flows are interbedded with green to reddish-brown metamorphosed volcanic breccia, thin beds of gray to purple phyllitic tuff and siltstone, and green to pink arkosic (containing quartz and feldspar) metamorphosed sandstone. Individual flows can range from 1 to 50 m (3 to 164 ft) thick and display columnar jointing, vesicular flow margins, porphyritic units, and stratigraphic separation by volcanic breccia or associated metamorphosed sedimentary rocks such as phyllite and quartz-sericite schist (Badger1992; Southworth and Denenny 2006). The overall thickness of the Catoctin Formation is estimated at 600 m (2,000 ft) (Mitra 1989).

This approximation is based on measurements of a location south of the park where a nearly complete section forms a prominent ledge.

Original stratigraphic relationships remain preserved in the flows, despite pervasive metamorphism. The greenstone consists of as many as ten distinct volcanic flows at several locations along the Blue Ridge-South Mountain anticlinorium. The lack of erosional nonconformities and thick interbeds of metamorphosed sedimentary rock suggests that the overall eruption time was relatively short. Badger (1992) suggests an active flow duration of approximately 3 to 5 million years. This timeframe is analogous to the Columbia River Basalts in Washington and Oregon. The thin (1 m [3 ft]) interbeds of phyllite are of igneous origin, but possibly from a separate, more felsic source than the Catoctin metamorphosed basalt flows (Badger 1992).

Of the rocks exposed within the park, the dark bluish-black, fine-grained metamorphosed rhyolite (or metarhyolite) from the Catoctin Formation is the oldest rock that has been dated using radioactive isotopes. Uranium-lead (U-Pb) dating on zircon minerals yielded an age of 560 million years (Southworth and Denenny 2006, with data from Aleinikoff, written communication 2005). This metarhyolite was ideal for producing early stone implements. It crops out within the park on the hills and creek valley along Foxville-Deerfield Road (Southworth and Denenny 2006).

The entire volcanic sequence of the Catoctin Formation is interpreted as the remnants of continental flood basalt erupted during the opening of the Iapetus Ocean in the Late Precambrian (Neoproterozoic). Tensional settings such as continental rifts, where the Earth's crust is pulled apart, caused a focused decrease in pressure below the Earth's surface, which caused local melting and upwelling of mantle material. This resulted in basaltic volcanism and produced enough material to accumulate over 11,000 km^2 (4,247 mi^2) of flood basalt at approximately 570 million years (Ma). This would be the largest flood basalt province in eastern North America (Badger 1992). The Catoctin flows are normally assumed to be of subaerial origin based on the originally tholeiitic composition of the lavas, the scoriaceous nature of many flows, and the common occurrence of columnar jointing. However, pillow structures also suggest at least a partial subaqueous origin for the flows (Mitra 1989).

Columnar Weathering and Stone Streams

Several outcrops of folded and faulted metamorphic rocks are scattered throughout the park. These rocks can dip nearly vertical in some areas. Cross and longitudinal joints and fractures formed during regional folding. These open structures influence modern drainage patterns and experience preferential weathering (Southworth and Denenny 2006). The rock breaks down in a unique way, causing distinct columns of rock to remain standing, isolated from neighboring slopes when exposed to weathering (including the wedging action of water in cracks, joints, and fractures). Melt water from

snow trickles through cracks in the rock and freezes at night during the colder months. The expansion of the ice in the cracks works in concert with tree and plant roots to wedge the rocks apart. Gravity is the largest component to the formation of tors (high isolated pinnacles) and blocks on ridge tops (Southworth, written communication 2009). Weathered gray Weverton Formation quartzite interbedded with metamorphosed siltstone of the Maryland Heights Member comprises Chimney Rock and Wolf Rock at elevations of 433 m (1,419 ft) and 430 m (1,401 ft), respectively (figs. 4 and 5) (Southworth and Denenny 2006). Weathered Catoctin greenstone forms Hog Rock.

Ice wedging was especially active during the periglacial (influenced by cold temperatures associated with continental glaciers) conditions of the Pleistocene Epoch. Thousands of boulders and smaller rocks littered the bases of rock outcrops as talus and, when caught up in a water-saturated mass, slid down the slopes along frozen layers of ground in a process known as solifluction (fig. 6) (Means 1995). Stony remnants now litter the slopes of Catoctin Mountain. Many of the stone flows are preserved today as "stone streams" whether or not water flows over them.

Catoctin Mountain Park contains three basic types of stone streams: (1) boulder-covered slopes; (2) side-slope stone streams; and (3) valley-bottom stone streams. Boulder-covered slopes are classified as areas covered by boulders that are up to 6 m (20 ft) long and spaced less than 15 m (50 ft) apart. Boulders contained on these slopes are often of the Weverton Formation and are found near Chimney Rock, Wolf Rock, and the slope down to Owens Creek.

Side-slope stone streams are linear deposits approximately 15 to 152 m (50 to 500 ft) across and up to 0.8 km (0.5 mi) long. At their heads is typically a scarp or outcrop of the Weverton Formation (Means 1995). Boulders in side-slope stone streams average 1 m (3 ft) in length, are spaced less than 0.6 m (2 ft) apart, and may be as much as 3 m (11 ft) long. Side-slope stone streams are visible below the Catoctin Park Administrative Office and appear to be "flowing" into Big Hunting Creek (fig. 7). Other examples are along the trail to Chimney Rock, upstream from the parking lot across Route 77 from the Administrative Office, and 0.4 km (0.25 mi) below the office (just past the right angle bend in the creek, from the Bear Branch bridge) (Means 1995).

Valley-bottom stone streams are linear deposits of boulders that cover stream bottoms as lag deposits after the streams have removed the fine material (Means 1995; Southworth, written communication 2009). These deposits are typical of the Big Hunting Creek bed (Means 1995). Identifying these features is tricky because large stones litter many stream bottoms. The angular nature (typical of frost wedging) and size of the boulders differentiate them from typical alluvial boulders that tend to be smoother and more rounded.

Geology and Archeology Connection

The Catoctin Formation contains local bodies of dark bluish-black metarhyolite (Southworth and Denenny 2006). These rocks began as silica-rich volcanics between basaltic flows. The locations of most of the wells and springs in the park coincide with these metarhyolites (Trombley and Zynjuk 1985). Springs served as important sources of water for settlers and American Indians. However, tool making is more significantly associated with the metarhyolite in the Catoctin Formation. Because of its fine-grained homogenous nature, metarhyolite was an excellent stone for arrowheads, knifes, scrapers, and other implements. The abundance of silica in the rock makes it a tough material as well. Just north of the park in southern Pennsylvania, Archaic age (8,000 to 1,200 B.C.E. [Before Common Era]) quarries have been found in the same metarhyolite rock unit that runs through the western portion of Catoctin Mountain Park (Means 1995). Catoctin experienced a very active period in stone quarrying between 200 and 900 C.E. (Common Era). Tools fashioned from this unique rock were found as far away as the eastern shore of Chesapeake Bay. This lends credence to its worth and the extent to which it was traded among early tribes.

Hunting tools and animal (mastodon) teeth in Frederick County represent local ancient American Indian activity. Early settlers reported an Indian hunting camp northwest of Frederick (Means 1995). The area provided American Indians with materials for tools; animals for food and clothing; and a variety of nuts, berries, and other plants for gathering.

Geology and Historical Preservation

One of the major goals of the park is to preserve the historical context of the area; this includes preserving and restoring old buildings and the landscape around them (fig. 8). Maintaining this landscape often means resisting natural geologic changes, which presents several management challenges. Geologic slope processes such as landsliding, slumping, chemical weathering, block sliding, and slope creep are constantly changing the landscape at the park. Runoff erodes sediments from many open areas and carries them down streams and gullies. Erosion naturally diminishes higher areas and fills in the lower areas to distort the historical context of the landscape.

The history of the area is heavily influenced by its geology. The ridges and valleys made travel parallel to their trend easy and traversing their trend difficult. Many small valleys remained isolated until reliable roads were built. Ore from the iron-rich minerals hematite and limonite was discovered in the 1770s, and Catoctin Furnace was constructed in 1776 for the extraction of so-called "pig" ore. Remnants of the original 1776 Catoctin

Furnace are present in nearby Cunningham Falls State Park. The charcoal needed to fuel the ore-producing furnace was on hand on the nearby slopes of Catoctin Mountain. Thousands of acres of climax hardwood forest fell to produce iron for stoves, wheels, cannons, cannonballs, and steamboat parts, and according to some sources, plates for the iron clad Civil War vessel USS *Monitor* (although Wehrle 2000 suggests this is unlikely). The local geology dictated where this production would occur.

Catoctin Mountain provided thickly forested slopes, abundant fresh running water (for washing ore and providing mechanical power), limestone for calcium carbonate (necessary for iron extraction), and abundant high-grade iron ore deposits. Iron ore (hematite and limonite) was from the Chilhowee Group strata between the Harpers Formation and the Frederick Limestone (S. Southworth, written communication, 2009).

The furnace ceased operation in 1903, leaving the landscape barren, deforested, and abandoned. Its renaissance was in the 1930s when the federal government purchased, reforested, developed, and restored many acres. Several features of the park, the forests not included, are remnants of this time. Buildings and developments (some listed on the National Register of Historic Places)—such as Camp Misty Mount, the Round Meadow blacksmith shop, the Blue Blazes Contact Station (now the visitor center), Camp Greentop, Round Meadow, and Camp Hi-Catoctin (now closed to the public as the presidential retreat Camp David)—were erected by the WPA and CCC in the 1930s and 1940s. Work also included construction and improvement of roads (Park Central Road), trails, stream restoration, and water systems (Means 1995).

These historic structures are all vulnerable to change due to the geologic processes of weathering and erosion. Balancing the need to let nature take its course and to preserve features in that course is a constant struggle because the goal of the park is to preserve both the natural and historical settings. This goal is under constant pressure by both the continuous natural processes of erosion and weathering and the demands of an increasing local population and urban development.

Issues also arise from opposing values between cultural and natural resource management. For example, a proposal for restoration of a historic building may consist of removing surrounding natural resources or planting exotics. The streams in the park are also sometimes changed to preserve fishing habitat and to protect trails, buildings, and streambanks from being undercut. These efforts attempt to stop or reverse many natural geologic processes.

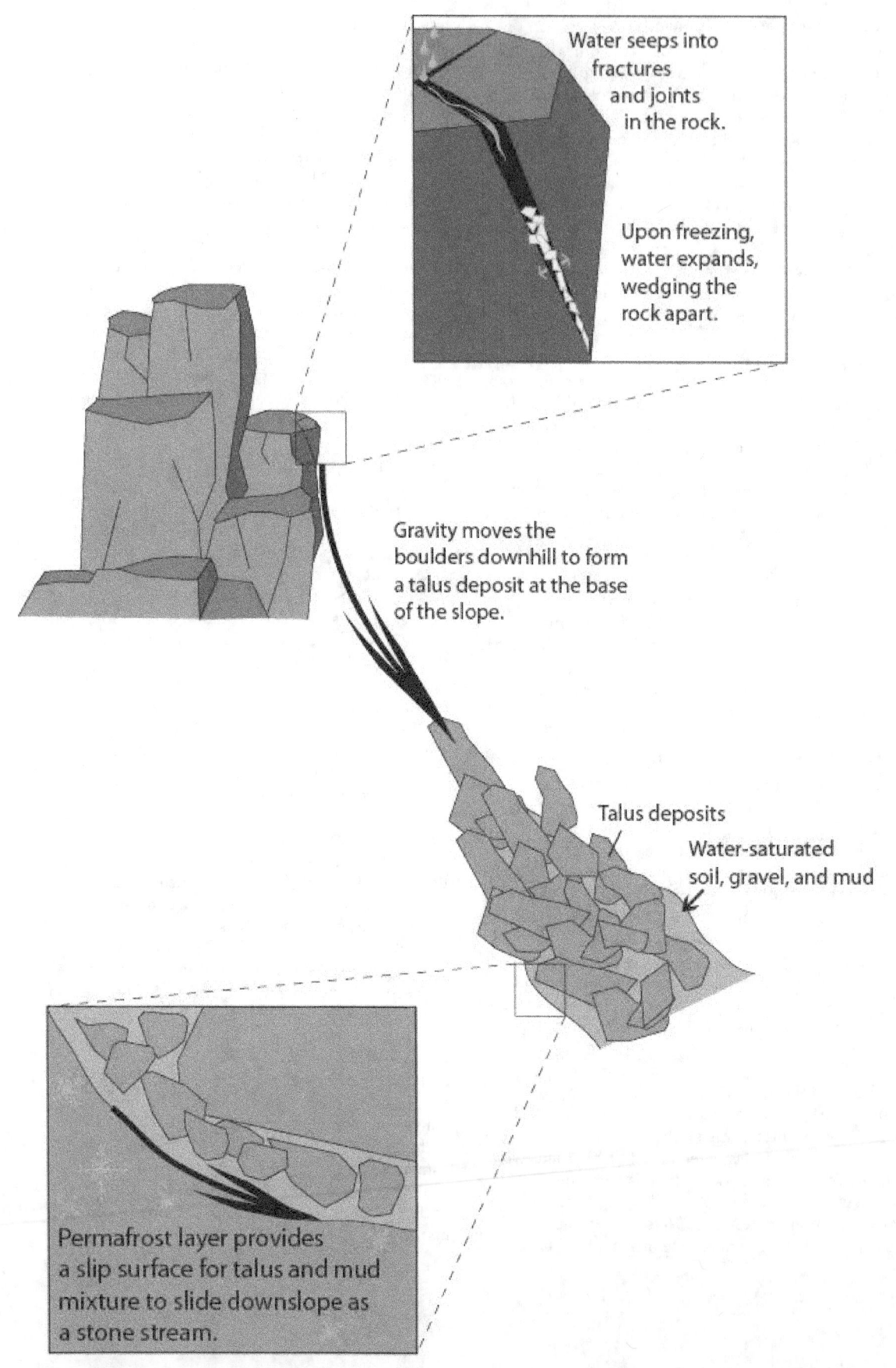

Water seeps into fractures and joints in the rock.

Upon freezing, water expands, wedging the rock apart.

Gravity moves the boulders downhill to form a talus deposit at the base of the slope.

Talus deposits

Water-saturated soil, gravel, and mud

Permafrost layer provides a slip surface for talus and mud mixture to slide downslope as a stone stream.

Figure 6. Diagram showing frost-wedge weathering and subsequent formation of stone streams in a typical outcrop (Chimney Rock) at Catoctin Mountain Park. Graphic is by Trista L. Thornberry-Ehrlich (Colorado State University).

Figure 7. A stone stream (arrows) near Big Hunting Creek, below the Catoctin Mountain Park administrative office. Ice wedging and subsequent solifluction (see Fig. 6) during the Pleistocene produced these features, visible in many areas within the park. NPS Photo courtesy Sean Denniston (NPS-CATO).

Figure 8. Cabin at Camp Misty Mount, one of several projects completed during the New Deal programs of the 1930s. The WPA built the camp in 1937. NPS Photo.

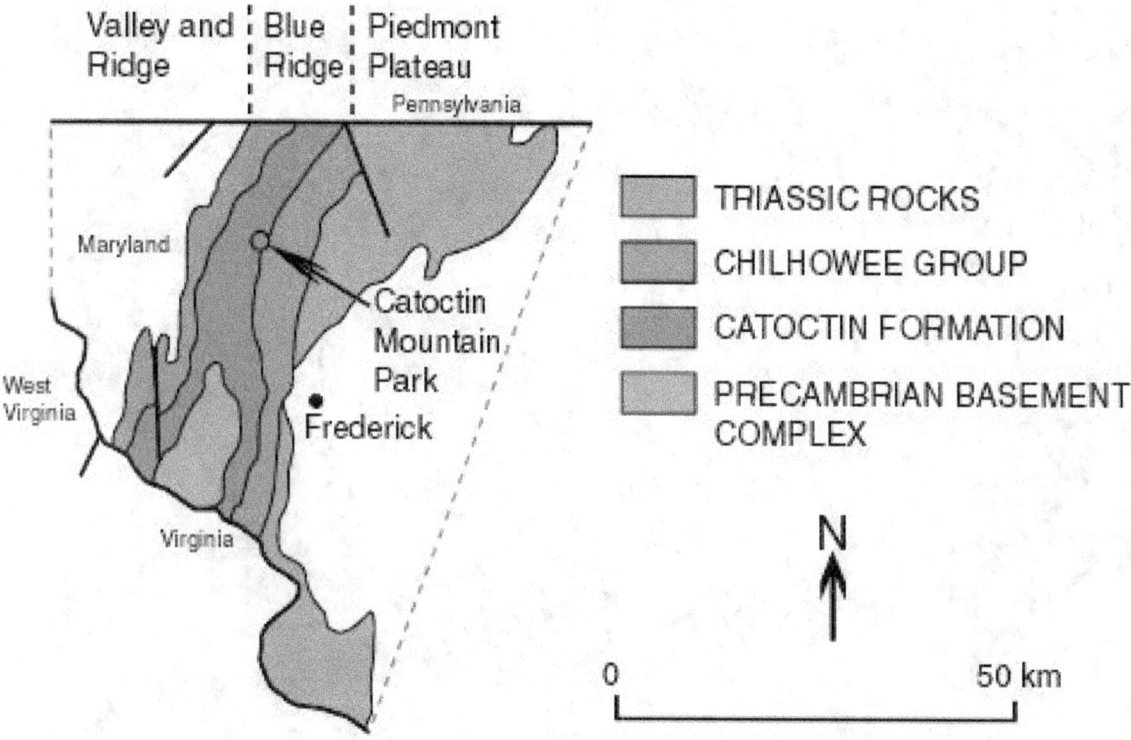

Figure 9. Index map of the Catoctin Formation relative to other units in the Blue Ridge portion of Maryland. Pre-Catoctin sedimentary rock units such as the Swift Run, Mechum River, and Fauquier formations are not represented at this map scale, but would locally exist farther south between the Catoctin Formation and the Precambrian Basement Complex units. Graphic adapted from Badger (1992).

Map Unit Properties

This section identifies characteristics of map units that appear on the Geologic Resources Inventory digital geologic map of Catoctin Mountain Park. The accompanying table is highly generalized and for background purposes only. Ground-disturbing activities should not be permitted or denied on the basis of information in this table.

The map units in the Catoctin Mountain Park area can be broken into several groups based on their age and lithology (mineral assemblage) (fig. 9). The oldest rocks in the area are the Precambrian granodiorite and biotite granite gneiss. These do not crop out within the park, but are locally intruded by feeder dikes of Catoctin Formation metamorphosed basalt or greenstone. Locally, the Catoctin Formation directly overlies the Precambrian granodiorite and biotite granite gneiss. Elsewhere, however (south of the park), the Late Precambrian-Early Cambrian Swift Run Formation overlies the Precambrian gneiss on the west limb of the Blue Ridge-South Mountain anticlinorium, whereas on the east limb, the Mechums River and Fauquier formations overlie the Precambrian gneisses. In the park, these formations do not crop out beneath the Catoctin Formation. The Catoctin Formation contains green, massive, and schistose metamorphosed basalt flows, and quartz-rich metarhyolite interlayered with tan phyllite and quartz-sericite schist (Southworth and Denenny 2006).

Deposited atop the older metamorphic rocks are the metamorphosed sedimentary rocks of the Chilhowee Group. Locally, the Chilhowee Group is composed of four formations, from oldest (lowest) to youngest (highest): (1)the Loudoun Formation (quartz and red jasper pebble conglomerate with tuffaceous phyllite); (2) the Weverton Formation (including quartzite, pebble conglomerate, metamorphosed graywacke, and metamorphosed siltstone); (3) the Harpers Formation (phyllite, metamorphosed siltstone, and metamorphosed sandstone); and (4) the Antietam Formation (quartzite with fossils). The Harpers, Loudoun, and Weverton formations appear on the geologic map (Southworth and Denenny 2006). The Loudoun Formation (transitional between the Catoctin Formation and rest of the Chilhowee Group) crops out on the south bank of Big Hunting Creek and along the slopes of the north side of Maryland Highway 77, east of the visitor center (Southworth and Denenny 2006; Southworth et al. 2007). The Weverton Formation crops out beneath the high ridge north of the visitor center and along the tail to Thurmont Vista. The Harpers Formation appears in outcrop along Big Hunting Creek in the easternmost portion of the park (Southworth and Denenny 2006).

In areas adjacent to Catoctin Mountain Park (notably in the valleys and outside the map area) are the Cambrian age Tomstown Dolomite and Frederick Limestone that were deposited atop the Chilhowee Group. Locally, Upper Cambrian to Lower Ordovician Grove Limestone is present as well as Triassic age rocks of the Newark Group. The Gettysburg Shale and New Oxford Formation lie within several Triassic extensional basins as part of the Newark Group. Scant diabase sills and dikes are late remnants of tectonic extension and renewed igneous activity in the area.

Lining river and stream valleys are unconsolidated terrace gravels, alluvial gravels, sands, and silts, in addition to colluvial slope deposits such as talus, angular stone streams, boulder fields, and slumps. These units are Quaternary age and cover much of the landscape at Catoctin Mountain Park. Quaternary terrace deposits are prevalent above local flood plains and consist of reworked alluvial sand, gravel, silt, and clay, as well as larger colluvium (Southworth and Denenny 2006). Flanking active streams are broad alluvial deposits consisting of gravel, sand, silt, and clay layers (Southworth and Denenny 2006). These unconsolidated deposits act as local aquifers.

Digital Geologic Map

Geologic maps facilitate an understanding of the Earth, its processes, and the geologic history responsible for its formation. Hence, the geologic map for Catoctin Mountain Park informed the "Geologic History," "Geologic Features and Processes," and "Geologic Issues" sections of this report. Geologic maps are essentially two-dimensional representations of complex three-dimensional relationships. The various colors on geologic maps illustrate the distribution of rocks and unconsolidated deposits. Bold lines that cross or separate the color patterns mark structures such as faults and folds. Point symbols indicate features such as dipping strata, sample localities, mines, wells, and cave openings.

Incorporation of geologic data into a Geographic Information System (GIS) increases the usefulness of geologic maps by revealing the spatial relationships to other natural resources and anthropogenic features. Geologic maps are indicators of water resources because they show which rock units are potential aquifers and are useful for finding seeps and springs. Geologic maps do not show soil types and are not soil maps, but they do show parent material, a key factor in soil formation. Furthermore, resource managers have used geologic maps to make connections between geology and biology; for instance, geologic maps have served as tools for locating sensitive, threatened, and endangered plant species, which may prefer a particular rock unit.

Although geologic maps do not show where earthquakes will occur, the presence of a fault indicates past movement and possible future seismic activity. Geologic maps do not show where the next landslide, rockfall, or volcanic eruption will occur, but mapped deposits show areas that have been susceptible to such geologic hazards. Geologic maps do not show archaeological or cultural resources, but past peoples may have inhabited or been influenced by various geomorphic features that are shown on geologic maps. For example, alluvial terraces may preserve artifacts, and formerly inhabited alcoves may occur at the contact between two rock units.

The geologic units listed in the following table correspond to the accompanying digital geologic data. Map units are listed in the table from youngest to oldest. Please refer to the geologic timescale (fig. 10) for the age associated with each time period. This table highlights characteristics of map units such as susceptibility to hazards; the occurrence of fossils, cultural resources, mineral resources, and caves; and the suitability as habitat or for recreational use.

The GRI digital geologic maps reproduce essential elements of the source maps including the unit descriptions, legend, map notes, graphics, and report. The following references are source data for the GRI digital geologic map for Catoctin Mountain Park:

Southworth, S., and D. Denenny. 2006. *Geologic Map of the National Parks in the National Capital Region, Washington, D.C., Virginia, Maryland and West Virginia*. Scale 1:24,000. Open File Report OF 2005-1331. Reston, VA: U.S. Geological Survey.

Southworth, S., D. K. Brezinski, A. A. Drake, Jr., W. C. Burton, R. C. Orndorff, A. J. Froelich, J. E. Reddy, D. Denenny, and D. L. Daniels. 2007. *Geologic Map of the Frederick 30' x 60' Quadrangle, Maryland, Virginia, and West Virginia*. Scale 1:100,000. Scientific Investigations Map 2889. Reston, VA: U.S. Geological Survey.

The GRI team implements a geology-GIS data model that standardizes map deliverables. This data model dictates GIS data structure including data layer architecture, feature attribution, and data relationships within ESRI ArcGIS software, increasing the overall quality and utility of the data. GRI digital geologic map products include data in ESRI personal geodatabase and shapefile GIS formats, layer files with feature symbology, Federal Geographic Data Committee (FGDC)-compliant metadata, a Windows help file that contains all of the ancillary map information and graphics, and an ESRI ArcMap map document file that easily displays the map and connects the help file directly to the map document. GRI digital geologic data are included on the attached CD and are available through the NPS Data Store (http://science.nature.nps.gov/nrdata/).

Map Unit Properties Table

Age	Unit Name (Symbol)	Features and Description	Erosion Resistance	Suitability for Development	Hazards	Paleontological Resources	Cultural Resources	Karst	Mineral Occurrence	Habitat	Recreation	Geologic Significance
QUATERNARY (HOLOCENE)	Alluvium (Qa)	Qa contains broad deposits flanking active stream channels of sand, gravel, clay, and silt layers.	Very low	Avoid stream edge/ riparian areas for heavy development, especially for wastewater treatment facilities due to proximity to water and high permeability	Qa is associated with stream banks and riparian zone areas, and may be unstable if exposed on a slope or water-saturated	Modern remains	May contain artifacts and/or settlement sites along major waterways	None	Sand, gravel, silt, clay	Riparian zones and burrow habitat	Qa is suitable for some trail development	Qa contains a record of modern stream valley development throughout the Quaternary
QUATERNARY (HOLOCENE & PLEISTOCENE)	Terrace deposits, low level (Qt)	Qt deposits are concentrated near stream confluences and contain reworked alluvial sand, gravel, silt, and clay, as well as larger colluvium clasts.	Very low	Avoid most terrace deposits for heavy development due to instability of slopes and high permeability	Unit is associated with stream edge slopes deposited by gravity and water	May contain modern remains and plant fragments (pollen?)	May contain artifacts and/or settlement sites along major waterways	None	Cobbles, gravel, sand	Forms upland areas, supporting larger trees and bushes with more soil development along waterways	Suitable for most recreation unless unstable slopes are present	Terrace units record the evolution of local waterways and changes in channel morphology
CAMBRIAN	Chilhowee Group, Harpers Formation (Ch); Chilhowee Group, Weverton Formation, Owens Creek Member (Cwo); Chilhowee Group, Weverton Formation, Maryland Heights Member (Cwm); Chilhowee Group, Weverton Formation, Buzzard Knob Member (Cwb)	Ch contains greenish- to brownish-gray phyllite and metamorphosed siltstone interbedded with light gray to brown thin metamorphosed sandstone. The Weverton Formation contains three members. The uppermost member contains dark gray quartzite and pebble conglomerate atop gray quartzite interbedded with metamorphosed siltstone. The basal member contains light gray metamorphosed graywacke, quartzite, metamorphosed arkose, and metamorphosed siltstone.	Moderate	Cleavage along bedding planes may be surfaces of weakness; intersecting joints in Weverton Formation may compromise rock unit strength	Cw is exposed along stream banks and may be prone to slumping and mass wasting	Burrows, including *Skolithos*, in Harpers Formation (possible trilobite remains?)	Historically, iron ore is an important economic resource. Units provided building material for many of the area's historic structures	Not enough carbonate locally present	Source of iron ore. Large quartz grains and magnetite; used as attractive building stones	Units support hardwood forests	Units may attract climbers to upland areas	Ch was deposited in a deltaic and tidal flat environment; Cw records an alluvial plan depositional setting
CAMBRIAN	Loudoun Formation, Conglomerate (Clc); Loudoun Formation, Phyllite (Clp)	The Loudoun Formation is composed of a basal conglomerate of dark variegated quartz (present as milky, gray, and dusky red) and red jasper clasts. Interlayered with the conglomerate are dark, variegated, tuffaceous phyllite that locally contains sand grains and vesicles (amygdules).	Moderately high	Phyllite layers are areas of weakness between more resistant massive quartzite and conglomeratic layers	Unit is commonly exposed on slopes and is prone to blockfall; phyllites may contain shrink-and-swell clays	None documented	Jasper may have provided trade-tool material for American Indians	Not enough carbonate locally present	Red jasper; amygdules	Units support hardwood forests	Unit may attract climbers to cliff areas	Formation represents fluvial channel and fan deposits derived from Zc; unit records the transition between volcanism and the fluvial environment at the beginning of the Cambrian

Age	Unit Name (Symbol)	Features and Description	Erosion Resistance	Suitability for Development	Hazards	Paleontological Resources	Cultural Resources	Karst	Mineral Occurrence	Habitat	Recreation	Geologic Significance
PROTEROZOIC EON (EDIACARAN)	Catoctin Formation, Metabasalt (Zc); Catoctin Formation, Metarhyolite (Zcr); Catoctin Formation, Porphyritic (Zcp)	Units are dominated by metamorphosed basalt flows (greenstone). Some metamorphosed rhyolite (metarhyolite; a quartz-rich volcanic rock) is present locally. Greenstones consist of green massive and schistose metamorphosed basalt flows containing vesicles. The metarhyolite layers appear dark bluish-black, fine-grained, and foliated, weathering to light gray slabs. Locally, layers of tan phyllite and quartz-sericity schist are interlayered with the metarhyolite.	Moderately high, depending on the degree of alteration	Intersections of bedding and flow cleavages in greenstones, as well as heavily altered zones, may be points of weakness in units	Rockfall possible where units are exposed on high angle slope; metarhyolite units can have dangerous sharp edges	None	Cryptocrystalline metarhyolite was a prized tool material for American Indians	None	Amygdules; secondary minerals filling vesicles; epidosite (quartz and epidote masses)	Units weather to produce calcium- and magnesium-rich orangish clayey soils	If present on cliffs, certain units may attract climbing interest; avoid heavily altered areas for recreational development	Unit records wide-spread volcanic activity following the Grenville Orogeny; zircon U-Pb SHRIMP age of ~560 Ma; metarhyolite has an age of 571 ± 4 Ma (U-Pb)

Geologic History

This section describes the rocks and unconsolidated deposits that appear on the digital geologic map of Catoctin Mountain Park, the environment in which those units were deposited, and the timing of geologic events that created the present landscape.

Catoctin Mountain Park is situated along the ridge that forms the boundary between the Blue Ridge and the Piedmont physiographic provinces in central Maryland. As such, it contains features that are intimately tied with the long geologic history of the Appalachian Mountains and the evolution of the eastern coast of the North American Continent. A regional perspective is presented here to connect the landscape and geology of the park to its surroundings.

The recorded history of the Appalachian Mountains begins in the Proterozoic (or Precambrian, see fig. 10). In the mid-Proterozoic, during the Grenville Orogeny, a supercontinent formed consisting of most of the continental crust in existence at that time, including North America and Africa. The sedimentation, high-temperature deformation, polyphase metamorphism, magmatism (the intrusion of igneous rocks) occurring during and after the orogeny, and volcanism are manifested in the metamorphic granite and gneiss in the core of the modern Blue Ridge Mountains (Harris et al. 1997; Tollo et al. 2004).

These rocks formed over a period of 100 million years and are more than 1 billion years old, making them among the oldest rocks known in this region. They were later uplifted, and thus exposed to erosive forces for hundreds of millions of years. Their leveled surface forms a basement upon which all other rocks of the Appalachians were deposited (Southworth et al. 2001). At Catoctin Mountain Park, these ancient rocks are buried beneath the Catoctin Formation and the Chilhowee Group, but are exposed in the Blue Ridge south of the park (Means 1995).

The late Proterozoic, roughly 800 to 600 million years ago, brought extensional rifting to the area. Another episode of extension, approximately 570 million years ago, created fissures through which massive volumes of basaltic magma were extruded (fig. 11A) (Tollo et al. 2004). This volcanic activity lasted millions of years and alternated between flood-basalt flows and ash falls that now compose the Catoctin Formation (Southworth and Denenny 2006). The volcanic rocks covered the granitic/gneissic basement in the Catoctin Mountains area.

Because of the tensional tectonic forces, the super-continent broke up and a sea basin formed that eventually became the Iapetus Ocean. This basin subsided and collected many of the sediments that would eventually form the Appalachian Mountains (fig. 11B). Some of the sediments were deposited as alluvial fans, large submarine landslides, and turbidity flows during the development of a tectonically passive margin

(Southworth et al. 2001; Tollo et al. 2004); these units preserve their depositional features. These early sediments are exposed on Catoctin Mountain, Short Hill–South Mountain, and Blue Ridge–Elk Ridge, and in areas within and surrounding the park as the Chilhowee Group (Loudoun, Weverton, Harpers, and Antietam formations) (Southworth et al. 2001).

Associated with the shallow marine setting along the eastern continental margin of the Iapetus Ocean were large deposits of sand, silt, and mud in near-shore, deltaic, barrier-island, and tidal-flat areas. Some of these are present in the Chilhowee Group in central Maryland, including the Harpers Formation and the Antietam Formation (Schwab 1970; Kauffman and Frey 1979; Simpson 1991). In addition, huge masses of carbonate rocks, such as the Cambrian Tomstown Dolomite and Frederick Limestone, as well as the Upper Cambrian to Lower Ordovician Grove Limestone, were deposited atop the Chilhowee Group. They represent a grand platform thickening to the east that persisted during the Cambrian and Ordovician periods (545 to 480 million years ago) and that forms the floors of Frederick and Hagerstown valleys (Means 1995).

Somewhat later—540, 470, and 360 million years ago—igneous granodiorite, pegmatite, and lamprophyre, respectively, intruded the sedimentary rocks. The rocks were buried for about 260 million years from the Cambrian to the Permian periods (Southworth and Denenny 2006). During several episodes of mountain building and continental collision (described below), the entire sequence of sediments, intrusive rocks, and basalt was deformed and metamorphosed into schist, gneiss, marble, slate, and migmatite (Southworth et al. 2000).

Taconic Orogeny

From Early Cambrian through Early Ordovician time, orogenic activity along the eastern margin of the continent began again. The Taconic Orogeny (approximately 440 to 420 million years ago in the central Appalachians) was a volcanic arc–continent convergence. Oceanic crust and the volcanic arc from the Iapetus Ocean basin were thrust onto the eastern edge of the North American continent. The Taconic Orogeny resulted in the closing of the ocean, subduction of oceanic crust during the creation of volcanic arcs within the disappearing basin, and the uplift of continental crust (Means 1995).

In response to the overriding plate thrusting westward onto the continental margin of North America, the crust bowed downwards to create a deep basin that filled with mud and sand eroded from the highlands to the east (fig. 11C) (Harris et al. 1997). This so-called Appalachian basin was centered on what is now West Virginia. These infilling sediments covered the grand carbonate platform, and are now represented by the shale of the Ordovician Martinsburg Formation (Southworth et al. 2001).

During the Late Ordovician, the oceanic sediments of the shrinking Iapetus Ocean were thrust westward onto other deep-water sediments of the western Piedmont along the Pleasant Grove fault. Sediments that would later become sandstone, shale, siltstone, quartzite, and limestone were then deposited in the shallow marine to deltaic environment of the Appalachian basin. These rocks, now metamorphosed, currently underlie the Valley and Ridge province west of Catoctin Mountain Park (Fisher 1976).

This shallow marine to fluvial sedimentation continued for a period of about 200 million years during the Ordovician through Permian periods, and resulted in thick layers of sediments. The source of the sediments was the highlands that were rising to the east during the Taconian orogeny (Ordovician) and the Acadian orogeny (Devonian).

Acadian Orogeny
The Acadian Orogeny (approximately 360 million years ago) continued the mountain building of the Taconic orogeny as the African continent drifted toward North America (Harris et al. 1997). Similar to the preceding Taconic Orogeny, the Acadian event involved collision of landmasses, mountain building, and regional metamorphism (Means 1995). This event was focused farther north than central Maryland.

Alleghanian Orogeny
Following the Acadian Orogeny, the proto-Atlantic Iapetus Ocean closed during the Late Paleozoic as the North American and African continents collided. This collision formed the Pangaea supercontinent and the Appalachian mountain belt we see today. This mountain-building episode, termed the Alleghanian Orogeny (approximately 325 to 265 Ma), is the last major orogeny that affected the Appalachians (fig. 11D) (Means 1995). The rocks were deformed by folds and faults to produce the Sugarloaf Mountain anticlinorium and the Frederick Valley synclinorium in the western Piedmont, the Blue Ridge-South Mountain anticlinorium (including the Catoctin Mountains), and the numerous folds of the Valley and Ridge province (Southworth et al. 2001). Many of the faults and folds accommodating orogenic stresses are exposed today in the landscape surrounding Catoctin Mountain Park (fig. 3).

During this orogeny, rocks of the Great Valley, Blue Ridge, and Piedmont provinces were transported along the North Mountain fault as a massive block (Blue Ridge–Piedmont thrust sheet) westward onto younger rocks of the Valley and Ridge (Harris et al. 1997; Southworth et al. 2007). The amount of crustal shortening was very large. Estimates of 20 to 50% shortening would amount to 125 to 350 km (80 to 220

mi) (Harris et al. 1997). The orogeny produced regional-scale folds such as the Blue Ridge-South Mountain anticlinorium that define the province (fig. 3) (Southworth et al. 2007).

Deformed rocks in the eastern Piedmont were also folded and faulted, and existing thrust faults were reactivated as both strike-slip and thrust faults during the Alleghanian Orogeny (Southworth et al. 2001). Paleoelevations of the Alleghanian Mountains are estimated at approximately 6,000 m (20,000 ft), analogous to the modern-day Himalaya Range in Asia. These mountains have been beveled by erosion to elevations of less than 600 m (2,000 ft) west of Catoctin Mountain Park, about 10% of their previous elevations (Means 1995).

Triassic Extension to the Present
Following the Alleghanian Orogeny, during the Late Triassic, a period of rifting began as the deformed rocks of the joined continents began to break apart from about 230 to 200 million years ago. The supercontinent Pangaea was segmented into roughly the same continents that persist today. This episode of rifting, or crustal fracturing, initiated the formation of the current Atlantic Ocean and caused many block-fault basins to develop with accompanying volcanism (fig. 11E) (Harris et al. 1997; Southworth et al. 2001).

The Newark-Gettysburg Basin system is a large component of this tectonic setting. Large streams carried debris shed from the uplifted Blue Ridge and Piedmont provinces, creating alluvial fans at their mouths. These were deposited as non-marine mud and sand in fault-created troughs, such as the Frederick Valley in central Maryland and the Culpeper basin in the western Piedmont of central Virginia. Many of these rift openings became lacustrine basins and were filled with thick deposits of silt and sand.

The large faults, such as the border fault that lies east of Catoctin Mountain Park running beneath Thurmont and Catoctin Furnace, Maryland, formed the western boundaries of the basins and provided an escarpment that was quickly covered with eroded debris (Southworth and Denenny 2006). Magma intruded into the new sandstone and shale strata as sills (sub-horizontal sheets) and nearly vertical dikes that extend beyond the basins into adjacent rocks. After emplacement of this magma approximately 200 million years ago, the region underwent a period of slow uplift and erosion. The uplift was in response to isostatic adjustments (changes in crustal buoyancy) within the crust, which forced the continental crust upwards and exposed it to erosion.

Thick deposits of unconsolidated gravel, sand, and silt were shed from the eroded mountains. These were deposited at the base of the mountains as alluvial fans and spread eastward to be part of the Atlantic Coastal Plain (Duffy and Whittecar 1991; Whittecar and Duffy 2000; Southworth et al. 2001). The immense amount of material that was deposited has been inferred from the now-exposed metamorphic rocks. Many of the rocks exposed at the surface must have been at least 20 km (approximately 10 mi) below the surface prior to regional uplift and erosion. The erosion continues today with the Potomac, Rappahannock, Rapidan, Monocacy, and Shenandoah rivers, and tributaries stripping the Coastal Plain sediments, lowering the mountains, and depositing alluvial terraces along the rivers, creating the present landscape (fig. 11F).

Since the breakup of Pangaea and the uplift of the Appalachian Mountains, the North American plate has continued to move toward the west. The isostatic adjustments that uplifted the continent after the Alleghanian Orogeny continued at a lesser rate throughout the Cenozoic Era (Harris et al. 1997).

The landscape and geomorphology of the greater Potomac River Valley, including Big Hunting and Owens creeks, are the result of erosion and deposition from about the mid-part of the Cenozoic Period to the present, or at least the past 5 million years. The distribution of flood plain alluvium and ancient fluvial terraces of the rivers and adjacent tributaries reflect the historical development of both drainage systems. There is little or no evidence that the rivers migrated laterally across a broad, relatively flat region. It appears that the rivers have cut downward through very old resistant rocks, overprinting their early courses (Southworth et al. 2001). The steep ridges and ravines present at Catoctin Mountain Park attest to this downward cutting and overprinting.

Though continental glaciers from the Pleistocene ice ages never reached the central Maryland area (the southern terminus was in northeastern Pennsylvania), the colder climates of the ice ages played a role in the formation of the landscape at Catoctin Mountain.

Approximately 11,000 years ago, due to its position some 150 km (95 mi) south of the continental glacier in Pennsylvania, Catoctin Mountain experienced periglacial conditions that included discontinuous permafrost, tundra-like vegetation, and many freeze-thaw cycles per year because of the proximity to the glacial environment as well as the high elevation (Means 1995; Southworth and Denenny 2006). These freeze and thaw cycles led to the ice wedging of thousands of boulders and small rocks from the bedrock of the mountains. Daytime melt water would seep into cracks, freeze at night, expand, and drive the rocks apart. These stones slid down the slope as part of talus piles, and larger water-saturated masses slid over the partially frozen layer below in a process known as solifluction (fig. 6) (Means 1995). Frost wedging continues today contributing, for example, to the splitting of Wolf Rock (fig. 5).

Pleistocene ice age climate may have affected river valley morphology as well. The periglacial conditions that must have existed at high altitudes intensified weathering and other erosional processes (Harris et al. 1997). The landforms and deposits are likely late Tertiary to Quaternary, when a wetter climate, sparse vegetation, and frozen ground caused increased precipitation to run into the ancestral river channels, enhancing downcutting and erosion by waterways (Means 1995; Zen 1997a and 1997b). The water gap through the resistant Weverton Formation just below the park's administrative office is an example of such an incised waterway. The stream, while eroding through less resistant layers that once lay atop the Weverton, had a well-established channel that continued to cut through the very resistant quartzite. The water gap already existed when the layers above the quartzite eroded, leaving it as a ridge (Means 1995).

Eon	Era	Period	Epoch	Ma	Life Forms	North American Events
Phanerozoic	Cenozoic	Quaternary	Holocene	0.01	Modern humans	Cascade volcanoes (W)
			Pleistocene		Extinction of large mammals and birds	Worldwide glaciation
				1.8		
		Tertiary	Pliocene		Large carnivores	Sierra Nevada Mountains (W)
			Miocene	5.3	Whales and apes	Linking of North and South America
			Oligocene	23.0		Basin-and-Range extension (W)
				33.9		
			Eocene	55.8	Early primates	Laramide Orogeny ends (W)
			Paleocene			
				65.5		
	Mesozoic	Cretaceous			Mass extinction — Placental mammals — Early flowering plants	Laramide Orogeny (W) — Sevier Orogeny (W) — Nevadan Orogeny (W)
				145.5		
		Jurassic			First mammals	Elko Orogeny (W)
				199.6	Mass extinction	Breakup of Pangaea begins
		Triassic			Flying reptiles — First dinosaurs	Sonoma Orogeny (W)
				251		
	Paleozoic	Permian			Mass extinction — Coal-forming forests diminish	Supercontinent Pangaea intact — Ouachita Orogeny (S) — Alleghanian (Appalachian) Orogeny (E)
				299		Ancestral Rocky Mountains (W)
		Pennsylvanian			Coal-forming swamps — Sharks abundant — Variety of insects — First amphibians	
				318.1		
		Mississippian			First reptiles	
				359.2	Mass extinction	Antler Orogeny (W)
		Devonian			First forests (evergreens)	Acadian Orogeny (E-NE)
				416		
		Silurian			First land plants	
				443.7	Mass extinction	
		Ordovician			First primitive fish — Trilobite maximum — Rise of corals	Taconic Orogeny (E-NE)
				488.3		
		Cambrian				Avalonian Orogeny (NE)
					Early shelled organisms	Extensive oceans cover most of North America
				542		
Proterozoic		Precambrian			First multicelled organisms	Formation of early supercontinent — Grenville Orogeny (E)
					Jellyfish fossil (670 Ma)	First iron deposits — Abundant carbonate rocks
				2500		
Archean					Early bacteria and algae	
				≈4000		Oldest known Earth rocks (≈3.96 billion years ago)
Hadean					Origin of life?	Oldest moon rocks (4–4.6 billion years ago)
						Formation of Earth's crust
				4600	Formation of the Earth	

Age of Mammals (Cenozoic), *Age of Dinosaurs* (Mesozoic), *Age of Amphibians* / *Fishes* / *Marine Invertebrates* (Paleozoic)

Figure 10. Geologic time scale. Adapted from the U.S. Geological Survey (http://pubs.usgs.gov/fs/2007/3015/). Red lines indicate major unconformities between eras. Included are major events in life history and tectonic events occurring on the North American continent. Absolute ages shown are in millions of years (Ma, or mega-annum).

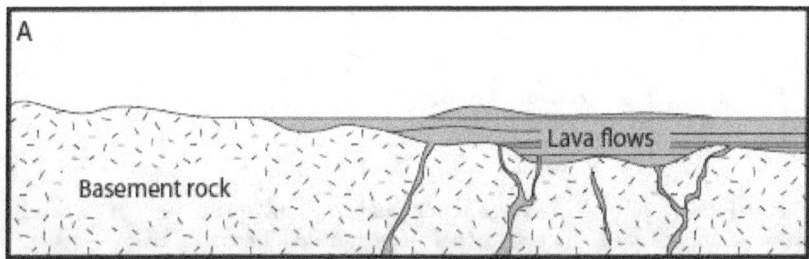

A

800-600 Ma—Following the Grenville orogeny and erosion, crustal extension leads to volcanism, producing flood basalt and ash flows.

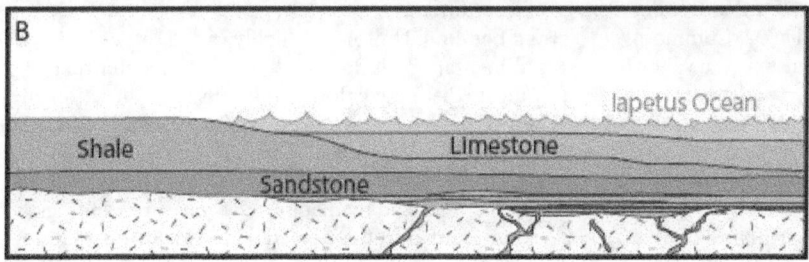

B

650-450 Ma—Iapetus Ocean continues to widen and the basin subsides; deposits of sand, silt, and clay, shed from the nearby highlands, and marine limestone fill the basin atop the flood basalt.

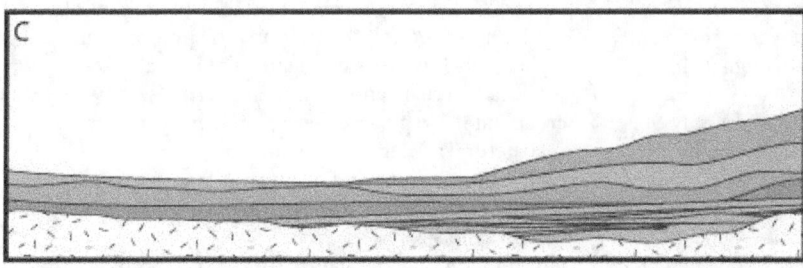

C

450-350 Ma—Inland-sea deposition continues as the Taconic and Acadian highlands rise to the east, providing more sediment.

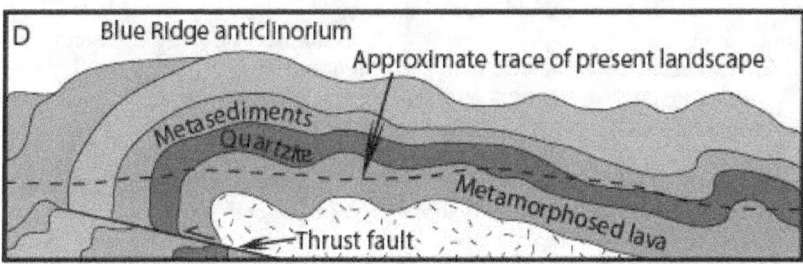

D

325-265 Ma—Alleghanian orogeny leads to metamorphism of the rocks, which are fractured, folded, and overturned to form high mountains over the present landscape.

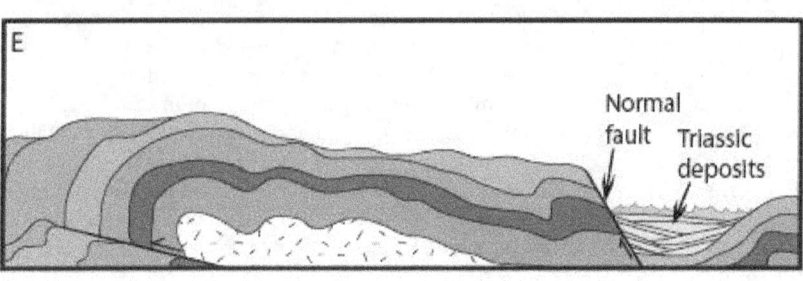

E

225-200 Ma—Following continental collision, the extensional environment creates fault-bounded basins along the eroding front of the mountain ranges, which provide sediment to the basins.

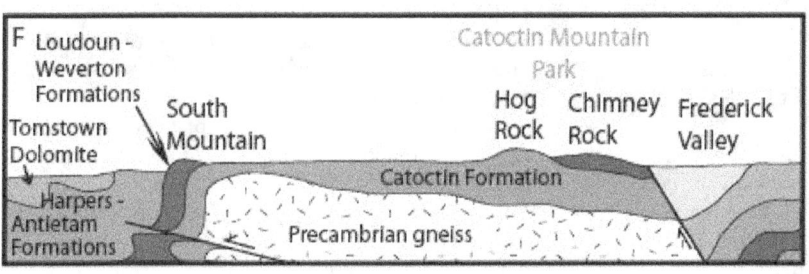

F

Present—Erosion bevels the mountains to the present topographic surface, deposition continues toward the eastern coast. and resistant rocks form local ridges.

Figure 11. Evolution of the landscape in the area of Catoctin Mountain Park from the Precambrian through the present. Graphic adapted from Means (1995). Ma, = millions of years (or mega-annum). Drawings not to scale.

Glossary

This glossary contains brief definitions of technical geologic terms used in this report. Not all geologic terms used are referenced. For more detailed definitions or to find terms not listed here please visit: http://wrgis.wr.usgs.gov/docs/parks/misc/glossarya.html.

allochthonous. Describing rocks or materials formed elsewhere than in their present location.

alluvial fan. A fan-shaped deposit of sediment that accumulates where a hydraulically confined stream flows to a hydraulically unconfined area. Commonly out of a mountain front into an area such as a valley or plain.

alluvium. Stream-deposited sediment that is generally rounded, sorted, and stratified.

anticline. A fold, generally convex upward, whose core contains the stratigraphically older rocks.

anticlinorium. A composite anticlinal structure of regional extent composed of lesser folds.

aquifer. A rock or sedimentary unit that is sufficiently porous that it has a capacity to hold water, sufficiently permeable to allow water to move through it, and currently saturated to some level.

basement. The undifferentiated rocks, commonly igneous and metamorphic, that underlie the rocks exposed at the surface.

basin (sedimentary). Any depression, from continental to local scales, into which sediments are deposited.

basin (structural). A doubly-plunging syncline in which rocks dip inward from all sides.

bed. The smallest sedimentary strata unit, commonly ranging in thickness from one centimeter to a meter or two and distinguishable from beds above and below.

bedding. Depositional layering or stratification of sediments.

block (fault). A crustal unit bounded by faults, either completely or in part.

breccia. A coarse-grained, generally unsorted sedimentary rock consisting of cemented angular clasts greater than 2 mm (0.08 in).

calcareous. Describing rock or sediment that contains calcium carbonate.

cementation. Chemical precipitation of material into pores between grains that bind the grains into rock.

chemical weathering. Chemical breakdown of minerals at the Earth's surface via reaction with water, air, or dissolved substances; commonly results in a change in chemical composition more stable in the current environment.

clastic. Describing rock or sediment made of fragments or pre-existing rocks.

clay. Can be used to refer to clay minerals or as a sedimentary fragment size classification (less than 1/256 mm [0.00015 in]).

conglomerate. A coarse-grained, generally unsorted, sedimentary rock consisting of cemented rounded clasts larger than 2 mm (0.08 in).

continental crust. The crustal rocks rich in silica and alumina that underlie the continents; ranging in thickness from 35 km (22 mi) to 60 km (37 mi) under mountain ranges.

convergent boundary. An active plate boundary where two tectonic plates are colliding.

craton. The relatively old and geologically stable interior of a continent.

cross-bedding. Uniform to highly varied sets of inclined sedimentary beds deposited by wind or water that indicate distinctive flow conditions (e.g., direction and depth).

cross section. A graphical interpretation of geology, structure, and/or stratigraphy in the third (vertical) dimension based on mapped and measured geological extents and attitudes depicted in a vertically oriented plane.

crust. The Earth's outermost compositional shell, 10 to 40 km (6 to 25 mi) thick, consisting predominantly of relatively low-density silicate minerals (also see "oceanic crust" and "continental crust").

crystalline. A regular, orderly, repeating geometric structural arrangement of atoms.

debris flow. A moving mass of rock fragments, soil, and mud, more than half the particles of which are larger than sand size.

deformation. A general term for the process of faulting, folding, and shearing of rocks as a result of various Earth forces such as compression (pushing together) and extension (pulling apart).

delta. A sediment wedge deposited at a stream's mouth where it flows into a lake or sea.

dike. A tabular, discordant igneous intrusion.

dip. The angle between a bed or other geologic surface and horizontal.

dip-slip fault A fault with measurable offset where the relative movement is parallel to the dip of the fault.

discordant. Having contacts that cut across or are set at an angle to the orientation of adjacent rocks.

drainage basin. The total area from which a stream system receives or drains precipitation runoff.

eustatic. Relates to simultaneous worldwide rise or fall of sea level.

extrusion. The emission of relatively viscous lava onto the Earth's surface, as well as the rock so formed.

extrusive. Of or pertaining to the eruption of igneous material onto the Earth's surface.

facies (metamorphic). The pressure-temperature regime that results in a particular, distinctive metamorphic mineralogy (i.e., a suite of index minerals).

facies (sedimentary). The depositional or environmental conditions reflected in the sedimentary structures, textures, mineralogy, fossils, etc. of a sedimentary rock.

fault. A break in rock along which relative movement has occurred between the two sides.

formation. Fundamental rock-stratigraphic unit that is mappable, lithologically distinct from adjoining strata, and has definable upper and lower contacts.

fracture. Irregular breakage of a mineral. Any break in a rock (e.g., crack, joint, fault).

frost wedging. The breakup of rock due to the expansion of water freezing in fractures.

geology. The study of the Earth, including its origin, history, physical processes, components, and morphology.

igneous. Describing a rock or mineral that originated from molten material. One of the three main classes of rocks—igneous, metamorphic, and sedimentary.

intrusion. A body of igneous rock that invades (pushes into) older rock. The invading rock may be a plastic solid or magma.

joint. A semi-planar break in rock without relative movement of rocks on either side of the fracture surface.

karst topography. Topography characterized by abundant sinkholes and caverns formed by the dissolution of calcareous rocks.

lacustrine. Pertaining to, produced by, or inhabiting a lake or lakes.

landslide. Any process or landform resulting from rapid, gravity-driven mass movement.

lava. Still-molten or solidified magma that has been extruded onto the Earth's surface though a volcano or fissure.

levees. Raised ridges lining the banks of a stream. May be natural or artificial.

limb. Either side of a structural fold.

lithosphere. The relatively rigid outmost shell of the Earth's structure, 50 to 100 km (31 to 62 miles) thick, that encompasses the crust and uppermost mantle.

mafic. Describing rock, magma, or mineral rich in magnesium and iron.

magma. Molten rock capable of intrusion and extrusion.

mantle. The zone of the Earth's interior between crust and core.

matrix. The fine grained material between coarse (larger) grains in igneous rocks or poorly sorted clastic sediments or rocks. Also refers to rock or sediment in which a fossil is embedded.

mechanical weathering. The physical breakup of rocks without change in composition. Synonymous with physical weathering.

member. A lithostratigraphic unit with definable contacts; a member subdivides a formation.

metamorphism. Literally, a change in form. Metamorphism occurs in rocks through mineral alteration, genesis, and/or recrystallization from increased heat and pressure.

mid-ocean ridge. The continuous, generally submarine, seismic, median mountain range that marks the divergent tectonic margin(s) in the Earth's oceans.

mud cracks. Cracks formed in clay, silt, or mud by shrinkage during subaerial dehydration.

normal fault. A dip-slip fault in which the hanging wall moves down relative to the footwall.

obduction. The process by which the crust is thickened by thrust faulting at a convergent margin.

oceanic crust. The Earth's crust formed at spreading ridges that underlies the ocean basins. Oceanic crust is 6 to 7 km (3 to 4 miles) thick and generally of basaltic composition.

orogeny. A mountain-building event.

outcrop. Any part of a rock mass or formation that is exposed or "crops out" at the Earth's surface.

overbank deposits. Alluvium deposited outside a stream channel during flooding.

Pangaea. A theoretical, single supercontinent that existed during the Permian and Triassic periods.

parent (rock). The original rock from which a metamorphic rock or soil was formed.

passive margin. A margin where no plate-scale tectonism is taking place; plates are not converging, diverging, or sliding past one another. An example is the east coast of North America. (also see "active margin").

pebble. Generally, small rounded rock particles from 4 to 64 mm (0.16 to 2.52 in) in diameter.

permeability. A measure of the relative ease with which fluids move through the pore spaces of rocks or sediments.

plate tectonics. The concept that the lithosphere is broken up into a series of rigid plates that move over the Earth's surface above a more fluid asthenosphere.

plateau. A broad, flat-topped topographic high (terrestrial or marine) of great extent and elevation above the surrounding plains, canyons, or valleys.

pluton. A body of intrusive igneous rock.

plutonic. Describes igneous rock intruded and crystallized at some depth in the Earth.

porosity. The proportion of void space (e.g., pores or voids) in a volume of rock or sediment deposit.

recharge. Infiltration processes that replenish groundwater.

regression. A long-term seaward retreat of the shoreline or relative fall of sea level.

relative dating. Determining the chronological placement of rocks, events, or fossils with respect to the geologic time scale and without reference to their absolute age.

reverse fault. A contractional high-angle (greater than 45°) dip-slip fault in which the hanging wall moves up relative to the footwall (also see "thrust fault").

rift valley. A depression formed by grabens along the crest of an oceanic spreading ridge or in a continental rift zone.

roundness. The relative amount of curvature of the "corners" of a sediment grain, especially with respect to the maximum radius of curvature of the particle.

sandstone. Clastic sedimentary rock of predominantly sand-sized grains.

scarp. A steep cliff or topographic step resulting from displacement on a fault, or by mass movement, or erosion.

scoriaceous. Describing an igneous rock with relatively large voids, formed when gas bubbles were trapped as the lava solidified.

seafloor spreading. The process by which tectonic plates diverge and new lithosphere is created at oceanic ridges.

sediment. An eroded and deposited, unconsolidated accumulation of rock and mineral fragments.

sequence. A major informal rock-stratigraphic unit that is traceable over large areas and defined by a major sea level transgression-regression sediment package.

shale. A clastic sedimentary rock made of clay-sized particles that exhibit parallel splitting properties.

silt. Clastic sedimentary material intermediate in size between fine-grained sand and coarse clay (1/256 to 1/16 mm [0.00015 to 0.002 in]).

siltstone. A variably lithified sedimentary rock composed of silt-sized grains.

slope. The inclined surface of any geomorphic feature or rational measurement thereof. Synonymous with gradient.

slump. A generally large, coherent mass movement with a concave-up failure surface and subsequent backward rotation relative to the slope.

soil. Surface accumulation of weathered rock and organic matter capable of supporting plant growth and commonly overlying the parent rock from which it formed.

solifluction. Slow flow of water-saturated soil down a steep slope that occurs in periglacial environments.

spring. A site where water issues from the surface due to the intersection of the water table with the ground surface.

strata. Tabular or sheetlike masses or distinct layers of rock.

stratigraphy. The geologic study of the origin, occurrence, distribution, classification, correlation, and age of rock layers, especially sedimentary rocks.

strike. The compass direction of the line of intersection of an inclined surface with a horizontal plane.

strike-slip fault. A fault with measurable offset where the relative movement is parallel to the strike of the fault.

subduction zone. A convergent plate boundary where oceanic lithosphere descends beneath a continental or oceanic plate and is carried down into the mantle.

subsidence. The gradual sinking or depression of part of the Earth's surface.

syncline. A downward curving fold with layers that dip inward, in which the core contains the stratigraphically younger rocks.

synclinorium. A composite synclinal structure of regional extent composed of lesser folds.

tectonic. Relating to large-scale movement and deformation of the Earth's crust.

terraces (stream). Step-like benches surrounding the present floodplain of a stream due to dissection of previous flood plain(s), stream bed(s), and/or valley floor(s).

terrane. A region or group of rocks with similar geology, age, or structural style.

terrestrial. Relating to land, the Earth, or its inhabitants.

thrust fault. A contractional fault with a shallowly dipping fault surface (less than 45°) where the hanging wall moves up and over relative to the footwall.

topography. The general morphology of the Earth's surface, including relief and locations of natural and anthropogenic features.

trace (fault). The exposed intersection of a fault with the Earth's surface.

trace fossils. Sedimentary structures, such as tracks, trails, or burrows, that preserve evidence of organisms' life activities, rather than the organisms themselves.

transgression. Landward migration of the sea as a result of a relative rise in sea level.

trend. The direction or azimuth of elongation of a linear geologic feature.

uplift. A structurally high area in the crust, produced by movement that raises the rocks.

vesicle. A void in an igneous rock formed by a gas bubble trapped as the lava solidified.

volcanic. Related to volcanoes. Igneous rock crystallized at or near the Earth's surface (e.g., lava).

water table. The upper surface of the saturated zone; the zone of rock in an aquifer saturated with water.

weathering. The set of physical, chemical, and biological processes by which rock is broken down.

References

This section lists references cited in this report, as well as additional references (indicated by an *) that may be of use to resource managers. A more complete geologic bibliography is available from the National Park Service Geologic Resources Division.

*Allen, R. M., Jr. 1963. *Geology and mineral resources of Greene and Madison counties.* Virginia Division of Mineral Resources Publication. Charlottesville, VA: Commonwealth of Virginia, Department of Conservation and Economic Development, Division of Mineral Resources.

Badger, R. 1992. Stratigraphic characterization and correlation of volcanic flows within the Catoctin Formation, central Appalachians. *Southeastern Geology* 32 (4): 175-195.

*Bloomer, R. O., and J. J. Werner. 1955. Geology of the Blue Ridge region in central Virginia. *Geological Society of America Bulletin* 66 (5): 579-606.

Bowser, C. J., and B. F. Jones. 2002. Mineralogic controls on the composition of natural waters dominated by silicate hydrolysis. *American Journal of Science* 302 (7): 582–662.

*Diecchio, R., and R. Gottfried. 2004. Regional Tectonic History of Northern Virginia. In *Geology of the National Capital Region–Field Trip Guidebook.* Circular 1264: 1-14. Reston, VA: U.S. Geological Survey.

Duffy, D. F., and G. R. Whittecar. 1991. Geomorphic development of segmented alluvial fans in the Shenandoah Valley, Stuarts Draft, Virginia. *Geological Society of America Abstracts with Programs* 23 (1): 24.

*D'Urso, G. J. 1981. An investigation of the Precambrian rocks of the Point of Rocks Quadrangle, Frederick County, Maryland and Loudoun County, Virginia. MS thesis, University of Pittsburgh.

Dyer, L. J., and W. S. Logan. 1995. Water-rock interaction and anthropogenic effects within the western Catoctin Mountain watershed, western Maryland. *Geological Society of America Abstracts with Programs* 27 (2): 51.

*Fish, T. W. 1974. Geology of the Catoctin Mountain-South Mountain Anticlinorium. MS thesis, Millersville University.

Fisher, G. W. 1976. The geologic evolution of the northeastern Piedmont of the Appalachians. *Geological Society of America Abstracts with Programs* 8 (2): 172–173.

Harris, A. G., E. Tuttle, and S. D. Tuttle. 1997. *Geology of National Parks.* Kendall/Hunt Publishing Company.

Katz, B. G., O. P. Bricker, and M. M. Kennedy. 1985. Geochemical mass-balance relationships for selected ions in precipitation and stream water, Catoctin Mountains, Maryland. *American Journal of Science* 285: 931-962.

Kauffman, M. E., and E. P. Frey. 1979. Antietam sandstone ridges; exhumed barrier islands or fault-bounded blocks? *Geological Society of America Abstracts with Programs* 11 (1): 18.

Logan, W. S., and L. J. Dyer. 1996. Influence of mineral weathering reactions, road salt and cation exchange on groundwater chemistry, Catoctin Mountain, central Maryland. *Geological Society of America Abstracts with Programs* 28 (7): 31–32.

Logan, W. S., and K. W. Kivimaki. 1998. Mass-balance modeling of dissolved solutes in groundwater of metasediments and basin fill sediments, eastern Catoctin Mountain, west-central Maryland. *Geological Society of America Abstracts with Programs* 30 (7): 375.

Matthews, E. D. 1960. *Soil survey of Frederick County, Maryland.* U.S. Department of Agriculture Soil Conservation Service.

Means, J. 1995. *Maryland's Catoctin Mountain parks; an interpretive guide to Catoctin Mountain Park and Cunningham Falls State Park.* Blacksburg, VA: McDonald & Woodward Publishing Company.

Mitra, G. 1989. Day four; The Catoctin Mountain–Blue Ridge anticlinorium in northern Virginia. In *Metamorphism and tectonics of eastern and central North America; Volume 2, Geometry and deformation fabrics in the Central and Southern Appalachian Valley and Ridge and Blue Ridge,* ed. P. M. Hanshaw, 31–44. Collection Field Trips for the 28th International Geological Congress.

Mitra, S. 1976. A quantitative study of deformation mechanisms and finite strain in quartzites. *Contributions to Mineralogy and Petrology* 59: 203-226.

*Nickelsen, R. P. 1956. Geology of the Blue Ridge near Harpers Ferry, West Virginia. *Geological Society of America Bulletin* 67 (3): 239–269.

*Nunan, W. E. 1980. Stratigraphy of the Weverton Formation, northern Blue Ridge Anticlinorium. PhD diss., University of North Carolina.

Onasch, C. M. 1986. Structural and metamorphic evolution of a portion of the Blue Ridge in Maryland. *Southeastern Geology* 26 (4): 229–238.

*Rice, K. C., M. M. Kennedy, C. A. Carter, R. T. Anderson, and O. P. Bricker. 1996. *Hydrologic and water-quality data for two small watersheds on Catoctin Mountain, north-central Maryland, 1987-93.* Open-File Report OF 95-0151. Reston, VA: U. S. Geological Survey.

*Rice, K.C., and O. P. Bricker. 1992. *Acid rain and its effect on streamwater quality on Catoctin Mountain, Maryland.* Open-File Report OF 92-0168. Reston, VA: U. S. Geological Survey.

Schwab, F. L. 1970. Origin of the Antietam Formation (late Precambrian?, lower Cambrian), central Virginia. *Journal of Sedimentary Petrology* 40 (1): 354–366.

Simpson, E. L. 1991. An exhumed Lower Cambrian tidal-flat; the Antietam Formation, central Virginia, U.S.A. In *Clastic tidal sedimentology.* eds. D. G. Smith, B. A. Zaitlin, G. E. Reinson, and R. A. Rahmani. Canadian Society of Petroleum Geologists Memoir 16: 123–133.

*Southworth, S., and D. K. Brezinski. 1996. *Geology of the Harpers Ferry Quadrangle, Virginia, Maryland, and West Virginia.* Bulletin B-2123. Reston, VA: U.S. Geological Survey.

Southworth, S., D. K. Brezinski, A. A. Drake, Jr., W. C. Burton, R. C. Orndorff, A. J. Froelich, J. E. Reddy, D. Denenny, and D. L. Daniels. 2007. *Geologic Map of the Frederick 30' x 60' Quadrangle, Maryland, Virginia, and West Virginia.* Scale 1:100,000. Scientific Investigations Map 2889. Reston, VA: U.S. Geological Survey.

Southworth, S., D. K. Brezinski, R. C. Orndorff, P. G. Chirico, and K. M Lagueux. 2001. *Geology of the Chesapeake and Ohio Canal National Historical Park and Potomac River Corridor, District of Columbia, Maryland, West Virginia, and Virginia.* CD-ROM (Disc 1: A, geologic map and GIS files; Disc 2: B, geologic report and figures). Open-File Report OF 01-0188. U.S. Geological Survey.

*Southworth, S., D. K. Brezinski, R. C. Orndorff, K. M. Lagueux, and P. G. Chirico. 2000. *Digital geologic map of the Harpers Ferry National Historical Park.* Open-File Report OF 00-0297. Reston, VA: U. S. Geological Survey.

Southworth, S., and D. Denenny. 2006. *Geologic Map of the National Parks in the National Capital Region, Washington, D.C., Virginia, Maryland and West Virginia.* Scale 1:24,000. Open File Report OF 2005-1331. Reston, VA: U.S. Geological Survey.

Southworth, S., C. Fingeret, and T. Weik. 2000. *Geologic Map of the Potomac River Gorge: Great Falls Park, Virginia, and Part of the C & O Canal National Historical Park, Maryland.* Open-File Report OF 00-264. Reston, VA: U.S. Geological Survey.

Tollo, R. P., C. M. Bailey, E. A. Borduas, and J. N. Aleinikoff. 2004. Mesoproterozoic Geology of the Blue Ridge Province and North-Central Virginia. In *Geology of the National Capital Region–Field Trip Guidebook.* Circular 1264: 17-75. Reston, VA: U.S. Geological Survey.

Trombley, T. J., and L. D. Zynjuk. 1985. *Hydrogeology and water quality of the Catoctin Mountain National Park area, Frederick County, Maryland.* Water Resources Investigations WRIR 85-4244. Reston, VA: U.S. Geological Survey.

Wehrle, E. F. 2000. *Catoctin Mountain Park: A Historic Resource Study.* National Park Service.

*Werner, H. J. 1966. *Geology of the Vesuvius Quadrangle, Virginia.* Report of Investigations. Charlottesville, VA: Virginia Division of Mineral Resources.

Whitaker, J. C. 1955. Geology of Catoctin Mountain, Maryland and Virginia. *Geological Society of America Bulletin* 66 (4): 435–462.

Whittecar, G. R., and D. F. Duffy. 2000. Geomorphology and stratigraphy of late Cenozoic alluvial fans, Augusta County, Virginia, U.S.A. In *Regolith in the Central and Southern Appalachians,* eds. G. M Clark, H. H. Mills, and J. S. Kite. *Southeastern Geology* 39 (3–4): 259–279.

Zen, E-an. 1997a. *The Seven-story river: Geomorphology of the Potomac River channel between Blockhouse Point, Maryland, and Georgetown, District of Columbia,* with emphasis on *The Gorge complex below Great Falls.* Open-File Report OF 97-60. Reston: VA: U.S. Geological Survey.

Zen, E-an. 1997b. *Channel geometry and strath levels of the Potomac River between Great Falls, Maryland, and Hampshire, West Virginia.* Open-File Report OF 97-480. Reston, VA: U.S. Geological Survey.

Appendix A: Geologic Map Graphic

The following page is a snapshot of the geologic map for Catoctin Mountain Park. For a poster-size PDF of this map or for digital geologic map data, please see the included CD or visit the Geologic Resources Inventory publications Web page (http://www.nature.nps.gov/geology/inventory/gre_publications.cfm).

Geologic Map of Catoctin Mountain Park

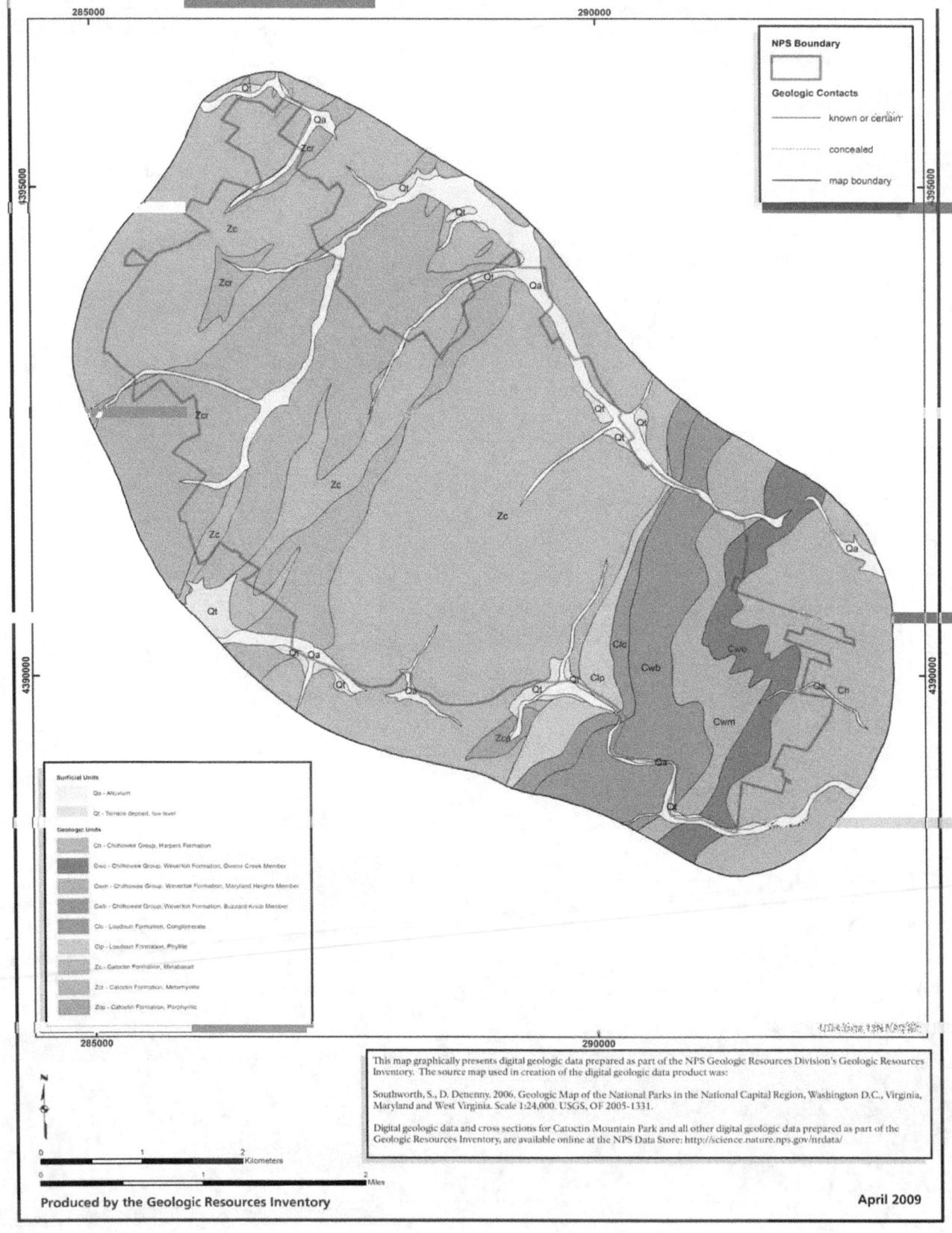

NPS Boundary

Geologic Contacts

known or certain

concealed

map boundary

Surficial Units

Qa - Alluvium

Qt - Terrace deposit, low level

Geologic Units

Ch - Chilhowee Group, Harpers Formation

Cwo - Chilhowee Group, Weverton Formation, Owens Creek Member

Cwm - Chilhowee Group, Weverton Formation, Maryland Heights Member

Cwb - Chilhowee Group, Weverton Formation, Buzzard Knob Member

Clc - Loudoun Formation, Conglomerate

Clp - Loudoun Formation, Phyllite

Zc - Catoctin Formation, Metabasalt

Zcr - Catoctin Formation, Metarhyolite

Zcp - Catoctin Formation, Porphyritic

This map graphically presents digital geologic data prepared as part of the NPS Geologic Resources Division's Geologic Resources Inventory. The source map used in creation of the digital geologic data product was:

Southworth, S., D. Denenny. 2006. Geologic Map of the National Parks in the National Capital Region, Washington D.C., Virginia, Maryland and West Virginia. Scale 1:24,000. USGS, OF 2005-1331.

Digital geologic data and cross sections for Catoctin Mountain Park and all other digital geologic data prepared as part of the Geologic Resources Inventory, are available online at the NPS Data Store: http://science.nature.nps.gov/nrdata/

N

0   1   2
Kilometers

0   1   2
Miles

Appendix B: Scoping Summary

The following excerpts are from the GRI scoping summary for Catoctin Mountain Park. The contact information and Web addresses in this appendix may be outdated. Please contact the Geologic Resources Division for current information.

Executive Summary

Geologic Resources Inventory (GRI) workshops were held for National Park Service (NPS) units in the National Capital Region (NCR) on April 30-May 2, 2001. The purpose was to view and discuss the park's geologic resources, to address the status of geologic mapping for compiling both paper and digital maps, and to assess resource management issues and needs. Cooperators from the NPS Geologic Resources Division (GRD), Natural Resources Information Division (NRID), individual NPS units in the region, and the United States Geological Survey (USGS) were present for the workshop.

The workshop involved half-day field trips to view the geology of Catoctin Mountain Park, Harpers Ferry NHP, Prince William Forest Park, and Great Falls Park, as well as another full-day scoping session to present overviews of the NPS Inventory and Monitoring (I&M) program, the GRD, and the on-going GRI. Round table discussions involving geologic issues for all parks in the National Capital Region included the status of geologic mapping efforts, interpretation, paleontologic resources, sources of available data, and action items generated from this meeting.

Overview of Geologic Resources Inventory

The emphasis of the inventory is not to routinely initiate new geologic mapping projects, but to aggregate existing "baseline" information and identify where serious geologic data needs and issues exist in the National Park System. In cases where map coverage is nearly complete (ex. 4 of 5 quadrangles for Park "X") or maps simply do not exist, then funding may be available for geologic mapping.

After introductions by the participants, Tim Connors presented overviews of the Geologic Resources Division, the NPS I&M program, the status of the natural resource inventories, and the GRI in particular.

He also presented a demonstration of some of the main features of the digital geologic database for the Black Canyon of the Gunnison NP and Curecanti NRA in Colorado. These have become the prototypes for the NPS digital geologic map model as it reproduces all aspects of a paper map (i.e., it incorporates the map notes, cross-sections, legend, etc.) with the added benefit of being geospatially referenced. It is displayed in ESRI ArcView shape files and features a built-in Microsoft Windows help file system to identify the map units. It can also display scanned JPG or GIF images of the geologic cross sections supplied with the map. Geologic cross section lines (ex. A-A') are subsequently digitized as a line coverage and are hyperlinks to the scanned images.

Joe Gregson further demonstrated the developing NPS Theme Manager for adding GIS coverage into projects "on-the-fly." With this functional browser, numerous NPS themes may be added to an ArcView project with relative ease. Such themes might include geology, paleontology, hypsography (topographic contours), vegetation, soils, etc.

Pete Chirico (USGS-Reston, VA) demonstrated the digital geology of Harpers Ferry and showed the group potential uses of a digital geologic coverage with his examples for Anacostia and Cumberland Island. The USGS also showed various digital products that they have developed for Chesapeake and Ohio Canal NHP and Great Falls.

GRBib

Individual Microsoft Word Documents of Geologic Bibliographies for each NCR park were distributed.

The sources for this compiled information are as follows:

- AGI (American Geological Institute) GeoRef,
- USGS GeoIndex, and
- ProCite information taken from specific park libraries.

These bibliographic compilations were then validated by GRI staff to eliminate problems that included duplicate citations and typographical errors and to check for applicability to the specific park.

After validation, they become part of a Microsoft Access database parsed into columns based on park, author, year of publication, title, publisher, publication number, and a miscellaneous column for notes.

From the Access database, they are exported as Microsoft Word Documents for easier readability, and eventually they are turned into PDF documents. They are then posted to the GRI website at; http://www2.nature.nps.gov/grd/geology/gri/products/geobib/ for general viewing.

Geologic Mapping

Existing Geologic Maps and Publications

A separate search was made after the bibliographies were assembled for any existing surficial and bedrock geologic maps for the National Capital Region parks. The bounding coordinates for each map were noted and entered into a GIS to assemble an index geologic map. Separate coverages were developed based on scales (*1:24,000*, *1:100,000*, etc.) available for the specific park. Numerous geologic maps at varying scales and vintages cover the area. Index maps were distributed to each workshop participant during the scoping session.

Status

The index of published geologic maps is a useful reference for the NCR. However, some of the maps are dated and in need of refinement. There is no existing large-scale coverage available for some areas.

The USGS began a project to map the Baltimore-Washington, D.C., area at 1:100,000 scale and learned that modern, large-scale geologic mapping for the NCR NPS areas would be beneficial to NPS resource management. The USGS subsequently developed a proposal to re-map the NCR at large scale (1:24,000 or greater) and to supply digital geologic databases to accompany this mapping. Scott Southworth (USGS-Reston, VA) is the project leader and main contact. The original Project Management Information Systems (PMIS) statement is available in Appendix C and on the NPS intranet (PMIS number 60900). The statement needs to be changed to reflect that the source of funding will be Inventory and Monitoring funds and *not* NRPP.

Desired Enhancements in the Geologic Maps for NCR Parks

To better facilitate the geologic mapping, Scott Southworth would like to obtain better topographic coverage for each of the NCR units. Tammy Stidham knows that some of these coverages are already available and will supply them to Scott and the USGS. In general, anything in Washington, D.C., proper has 1 meter topographic coverage and Prince George's County has 1:24,000 coverage.

Notes on Catoctin Mountain Park

Catoctin Mountain (CATO) will be a bigger project as there is an interesting surficial geologic story here. Base data are needed. Tammy says that at the time of the scoping meeting, there is not yet topographic data available, but hopefully data will be available by the time Scott gets there to map. James Voigt is concerned about poor forest regeneration and wonders if it is tied to the geology. The park would like to relate topographic aspect and the DEMs to the geology as well. There were discussions of trying to investigate the relationship of the purple fringed orchid habitat to underlying geology. The superintendent is concerned about potential geologic hazards that might be associated with climbing, as well as potential problems that may exist along Route 77 near Big Hunting Creek. Park staff would like to see better interpretive graphics pertaining to the geology to use in park brochures as well as at wayside exhibits in the park.

Digital Geologic Map Coverage

The USGS will supply digital geology in ArcInfo format for all of the NCR parks. GRI staff will take these data and add the Windows help file and NPS theme manager capability to the digital geology and will supply the results to the region to distribute to each park in NCR.

Other Desired Data Sets for NCR

Soils

Pete Biggam (GRD Soil Scientist) supplied the following information in reference to soils for parks:

National Capitol Parks - Central is covered by the "District of Columbia" Soil Survey (State Soil Survey Area ID MD099). It has been mapped and is currently being refined to match new imagery. An interim digital product is available to us via NRCS, but the "final certified" dataset most likely will not be available until FY03.

National Capitol Parks - Eastern is covered by portions of three soil survey areas: "District of Columbia" (MD099), "Charles County, Maryland" (MD017), and "Prince George's County, Maryland" (MD033). Both Charles County and Prince George's County are currently being updated, with Charles County scheduled to be available sometime in calendar year 2002, and Prince George's County sometime within calendar year 2003.

Paleontology

Greg McDonald (GRD Paleontologist) would like to see an encompassing, systematic paleontological inventory for the NCR describing the known resources in all parks with suggestions on how to best manage these resources. In addition to the parks containing paleo resources in NACE, according to his current database, the following are considered "paleo parks" in the NCR:

- Chesapeake & Ohio Canal NHP,
- George Washington Memorial Parkway,
- Manassas NBP,
- Prince William Forest Park, and
- Harpers Ferry NHP.

Geologic Report

A "stand-alone" encompassing report on each park's geology is a major focus of the GRI. As part of the USGS proposal to map the NCR, they will be summarizing the major geologic features of each park in a report to accompany their database. It was suggested that after the individual reports are finished, a regional physiographic report will be completed for the entire NCR.

NAME	AFFILIATION	PHONE	E-MAIL
Joe Gregson	NPS, Natural Resources Information Division	(970) 225-3559	Joe_Gregson@nps.gov
Tim Connors	NPS, Geologic Resources Division	(303) 969-2093	Tim_Connors@nps.gov
Bruce Heise	NPS, Geologic Resources Division	(303) 969-2017	Bruce_Heise@nps.gov
Lindsay McClelland	NPS, Geologic Resources Division	202-208-4958	Lindsay_mcclelland@nps.gov
Scott Southworth	USGS	(703) 648-6385	Ssouthwo@usgs.gov
Pete Chirico	USGS	703-648-6950	Pchirico@usgs.gov
Pat Toops	NPS, NCR	202-342-1443, ext. 212	Pat_toops@nps.gov
James Voigt	NPS, CATO	301-416-0536	Cato_resource_management@nps.gov
Marcus Koenen	NPS, NCR	202-342-1443, ext. 216	Marcus_koenen@nps.gov
Ellen Gray	NPS, NCR	202-342-1443, ext. 223	Ellen_gray@nps.gov
Dale Nisbet	NPS, HAFE	304-535-6770	Dale_nisbet@nps.gov
Suzy Alberts	NPS, CHOH	301-714-2211	Susan_alberts@nps.gov
Dianne Ingram	NPS, CHOH	301-714-2225	Dianne_ingram@nps.gov
Bill Spinrad	NPS, CHOH	301-714-2221	William_spinrad@nps.gov
Debbie Cohen	NPS, ANTI	301-432-2243	Debbie_cohen@nps.gov
Ed Wenschhof	NPS, ANTI/MONO	301-432-2243	Ed_wenschhof@nps.gov
Ann Brazinski	NPS, GWMP	703-289-2541	Ann_brazinski@nps.gov
Melissa Kangas	NPS, GWMP	703-289-2542	Melissa_Kangas@nps.gov
Barbara Perdew	NPS, GWMP	703-285-2964	Barbara_Perdew@nps.gov
Barry Wood	NPS, GWMP	703-289-2543	Barry_wood@nps.gov
Marie Sauter	NPS, CHOH	301-714-2224	Marie_frias@nps.gov
Carol Pollio	NPS, PRWI	703-221-2176	Carol_pollio@nps.gov
Duane Donnelly-Morrison	NPS, PRWI	703-221-6921	Duane_donnelly-morrison@nps.gov
Diane Pavek	NPS-NRS	202-342-1443, ext. 209	Diane_Pavek@nps.gov
Chris Jones	NPS-WOTR	703-255-1822	Christopher_Jones@nps.gov
Doug Curtis	NPS-NCR-NRS	202-342-1443, ext.228	Doug_Curtis@nps.gov
Brent Steury	NPS-NACE	202-690-5167	Brent_Steury@nps.gov
Dave Russ	USGS	703-648-6660	Druss@usgs.gov
Tammy Stidham	NPS-RTSC	202-619-7474	Tammy_stidham@nps.gov
Dan Sealy	NPS-GWMP	703-289-2531	Dan_Sealy@nps.gov
Sue Salmons	NPS-ROCR	202-426-6834, ext. 33	Sue_salmons@nps.gov

Catoctin Mountain Park
Geologic Resources Inventory Report

Natural Resource Report NPS/NRPC/GRD/NRR—2009/120

National Park Service
Acting Director • Dan Wenk

Natural Resource Stewardship and Science
Associate Director • Bert Frost

Natural Resource Program Center
The Natural Resource Program Center (NRPC) is the core of the NPS Natural Resource Stewardship and Science Directorate. The Center Director is located in Fort Collins, with staff located principally in Lakewood and Fort Collins, Colorado and in Washington, D.C. The NRPC has five divisions: Air Resources Division, Biological Resource Management Division, Environmental Quality Division, Geologic Resources Division, and Water Resources Division. NRPC also includes three offices: The Office of Education and Outreach, the Office of Inventory, Monitoring, and Evaluation, and Office of Natural Resource Information Systems. In addition, Natural Resource Web Management and Partnership Coordination are cross-cutting disciplines under the Center Director. The multidisciplinary staff of NRPC is dedicated to resolving park resource management challenges originating in and outside units of the National Park System.

Geologic Resources Division
Chief • Dave Steensen
Planning, Evaluation, and Permits Branch Chief • Carol McCoy
Geoscience and Restoration Branch Chief • Hal Pranger

Credits
Author • Trista Thornberry-Ehrlich
Review • Scott Southworth and Bruce Heise
Editing • Bonnie Dash
Digital Map Production • Stephanie O'Meara
Map Layout Design • Josh Heise

NPS 841/100133, August 2009